Getting Organized with Microsoft Lists

A User's Manual

Kiet Huynh

Table of Contents

Introduction

Microsoft Lists

1.1 The Importance of Organization

In today's fast-paced digital world, staying organized is more critical than ever. Whether you're managing personal tasks, coordinating team projects, or overseeing complex business operations, organization is the key to efficiency, productivity, and success. This section delves into the significance of organization, highlighting its benefits and the pivotal role it plays in various aspects of life and work.

1. Enhancing Productivity

Organization directly impacts productivity. When everything is in its place and easily accessible, you spend less time searching for information and more time focusing on tasks that matter. Microsoft Lists provides a structured way to manage data, ensuring that important details are always at your fingertips. By organizing your data into lists, you can quickly find and act on information, leading to faster decision-making and task completion.

For example, consider a project manager juggling multiple projects. With organized lists, they can track progress, assign tasks, and monitor deadlines efficiently. This not only boosts their productivity but also ensures that the entire team stays on track.

2. Improving Time Management

Time management is another area where organization proves invaluable. When tasks and responsibilities are clearly outlined and prioritized, it's easier to allocate time effectively. Microsoft Lists allows you to categorize and prioritize items, helping you manage your time better.

Think about a scenario where you're planning a major event. With Microsoft Lists, you can create a comprehensive checklist of tasks, set deadlines, and assign responsibilities. This organized approach ensures that nothing is overlooked, and every aspect of the event is managed within the stipulated time frame.

3. Reducing Stress and Overwhelm

Clutter, whether physical or digital, can lead to stress and a sense of overwhelm. When you're disorganized, tasks can pile up, deadlines can be missed, and important details can slip through the cracks. This can create a stressful work environment and affect your overall well-being.

Microsoft Lists helps alleviate this stress by providing a clear and organized view of your tasks and responsibilities. By breaking down complex projects into manageable lists, you can tackle each task one at a time, reducing the feeling of being overwhelmed.

4. Enhancing Collaboration

In a collaborative work environment, organization is essential for effective teamwork. When team members have access to organized lists, they can easily see their tasks, understand their priorities, and stay informed about project progress. This fosters better communication and collaboration.

For instance, in a marketing team working on a campaign, Microsoft Lists can be used to outline tasks such as content creation, social media scheduling, and performance tracking. Each team member can update their progress, ensuring that everyone is on the same page and working towards common goals.

5. Ensuring Accountability

Organization fosters accountability by clearly defining tasks and responsibilities. When roles and duties are outlined in an organized list, individuals know what is expected of them. This transparency promotes a sense of responsibility and ownership.

Consider a sales team using Microsoft Lists to manage leads and customer interactions. Each salesperson can be assigned specific leads to follow up on, with deadlines and notes recorded in the list. This organized approach ensures that every lead is accounted for and followed up on, enhancing accountability within the team.

6. Facilitating Goal Setting and Tracking

Setting and tracking goals is crucial for personal and professional growth. Organized lists provide a framework for defining, prioritizing, and tracking goals. With Microsoft Lists, you can create detailed plans, set milestones, and monitor progress.

For example, an individual aiming to improve their skills can use Microsoft Lists to outline a learning plan. They can list courses, books, and milestones, tracking their progress over time. This organized approach helps them stay focused and motivated.

7. Enhancing Decision Making

Access to organized information is vital for effective decision-making. When data is well-organized, you can quickly analyze it and make informed decisions. Microsoft Lists allows you to sort, filter, and view data in various ways, facilitating better analysis and decision-making.

Imagine a business owner evaluating sales performance. By organizing sales data in Microsoft Lists, they can easily identify trends, pinpoint areas for improvement, and make strategic decisions to boost sales.

8. Promoting Consistency and Standardization

Organization promotes consistency and standardization, which are essential for maintaining quality and efficiency. When processes and procedures are documented and followed consistently, it ensures that tasks are performed uniformly.

For instance, a company using Microsoft Lists to manage its onboarding process can ensure that every new employee goes through the same steps, receives the same information, and completes the same training. This consistency helps maintain high standards and a smooth onboarding experience.

9. Supporting Strategic Planning

Strategic planning involves setting long-term goals and defining the actions needed to achieve them. Organization is crucial for mapping out these plans and monitoring their execution. Microsoft Lists can be used to create detailed strategic plans, breaking down long-term goals into actionable steps.

Consider a nonprofit organization planning its annual fundraising campaign. By using Microsoft Lists to outline the campaign's goals, strategies, and actions, they can ensure that every aspect of the campaign is well-planned and executed effectively.

10. Enabling Continuous Improvement

Continuous improvement is a key aspect of personal and organizational growth. Organized lists provide a way to document processes, track performance, and identify areas for improvement. Microsoft Lists allows you to create and maintain records that support ongoing evaluation and enhancement.

For example, a customer service team can use Microsoft Lists to track customer feedback and complaints. By organizing this data, they can identify recurring issues, analyze trends, and implement improvements to enhance customer satisfaction.

Conclusion

The importance of organization cannot be overstated. It is the foundation of productivity, time management, stress reduction, collaboration, accountability, goal setting, decision-making, consistency, strategic planning, and continuous improvement. Microsoft Lists is a powerful tool that can help you achieve and maintain organization in all these areas.

By mastering Microsoft Lists, you can streamline your workflows, enhance your productivity, and achieve greater success in your personal and professional endeavors. This manual will guide you through the features and functionalities of Microsoft Lists, providing practical tips and insights to help you get organized and stay organized. Let's embark on this journey to mastering Microsoft Lists and unlocking the full potential of your organizational skills.

1.2 What is Microsoft Lists?

Microsoft Lists is a versatile and powerful application within the Microsoft 365 suite designed to help individuals and teams track information, organize work, and collaborate effectively. Launched in 2020, Microsoft Lists builds on the robust foundation of SharePoint Lists, adding enhanced features and a more user-friendly interface to meet modern organizational needs.

A Brief History

The concept of lists within Microsoft products isn't new. It dates back to the early days of SharePoint, which has long offered list functionality as a core component. SharePoint Lists allowed users to create, manage, and share lists within their organizations, providing a structured way to handle data and tasks. Microsoft Lists takes this concept further by providing a standalone application that integrates seamlessly with other Microsoft 365 apps like Teams, Outlook, and Power Automate.

Core Features

Microsoft Lists is packed with features that make it a valuable tool for various scenarios, from project management to inventory tracking. Here are some of the core features:

1. Customizable Templates: Microsoft Lists offers a range of ready-made templates to get you started quickly. These templates are tailored for specific use cases, such as issue tracking, asset management, event itineraries, and more. Each template provides a pre-configured structure that can be customized to fit your unique needs.

2. Rich Formatting: The application allows for rich text formatting, enabling users to highlight important information, add links, and include images within list items. This makes the data more engaging and easier to interpret.

3. Views and Filters: Lists can be viewed and filtered in multiple ways to make data more accessible and meaningful. Users can create custom views to display information in different formats, such as grids, calendars, and galleries. Filters can be applied to hone in on specific data points, making it easier to find what you need.

4. Integration with Microsoft 365: One of the standout features of Microsoft Lists is its deep integration with the Microsoft 365 ecosystem. Lists can be embedded in Teams channels, shared via Outlook, and connected to automation workflows through Power Automate. This integration streamlines processes and enhances collaboration.

5. Mobile Access: Microsoft Lists is accessible on mobile devices through dedicated apps for iOS and Android. This ensures that users can stay connected and manage their lists on the go, enhancing productivity regardless of location.

6. Collaboration Tools: Microsoft Lists supports real-time collaboration, allowing multiple users to edit and update lists simultaneously. Comments and @mentions can be used to facilitate discussions and ensure everyone is on the same page.

Use Cases

Microsoft Lists is incredibly versatile and can be used in a variety of scenarios across different industries. Here are some common use cases:

1. Project Management: Teams can use Microsoft Lists to manage project tasks, assign responsibilities, and track progress. The application's ability to integrate with Microsoft Teams makes it an ideal tool for collaborative project management.

2. Event Planning: Organizing events can be complex, but Microsoft Lists simplifies the process by providing templates for event itineraries, guest lists, and task assignments. Event planners can track every detail and ensure nothing is overlooked.

3. Asset Management: Companies can use Microsoft Lists to keep track of their assets, such as equipment, inventory, and office supplies. This helps in maintaining accurate records and ensuring efficient resource allocation.

4. Issue Tracking: For IT and customer support teams, Microsoft Lists can be used to track issues and support tickets. By documenting problems and their resolutions, teams can improve their response times and enhance service quality.

5. HR Management: Human resources departments can leverage Microsoft Lists to manage employee information, track job applications, and monitor training programs. This centralizes HR data and streamlines administrative tasks.

Key Benefits

The adoption of Microsoft Lists offers several key benefits to organizations:

1. Improved Organization: By providing a structured way to manage information, Microsoft Lists helps users stay organized and ensures that important data is easily accessible.

2. Enhanced Collaboration: The integration with Microsoft 365 and real-time collaboration features foster teamwork and make it easier for teams to work together effectively.

3. Increased Productivity: Automation capabilities and seamless integration with other Microsoft 365 apps reduce manual effort and streamline workflows, leading to increased productivity.

4. Flexibility and Customization: Microsoft Lists is highly customizable, allowing users to tailor lists to their specific needs. This flexibility makes it suitable for a wide range of applications.

5. Scalability: Whether you're a small team or a large enterprise, Microsoft Lists can scale to meet your needs. The application can handle large volumes of data and multiple users, making it a robust solution for growing organizations.

Getting Started

Starting with Microsoft Lists is straightforward, thanks to its intuitive interface and user-friendly design. Here's a quick overview of how to get started:

1. Accessing Microsoft Lists: Microsoft Lists is available to users with a Microsoft 365 subscription. It can be accessed via the Microsoft 365 app launcher or directly at lists.microsoft.com.

2. Creating a List: Once you're logged in, you can create a new list by selecting a template or starting from scratch. The application provides step-by-step guidance to help you set up your list and customize it to your needs.

3. Adding Data: After creating your list, you can start adding data by filling out the list items. The application supports various data types, including text, numbers, dates, and attachments.

4. Customizing Views: To make your data more manageable, you can create custom views that display information in different formats. This helps you focus on the most relevant data and improves usability.

5. Sharing and Collaborating: Microsoft Lists allows you to share your lists with colleagues and collaborate in real-time. You can set permissions to control who can view and edit your lists, ensuring data security and integrity.

6. Automating Workflows: By integrating with Power Automate, you can create automated workflows that streamline repetitive tasks. This saves time and reduces the risk of errors.

Conclusion

Microsoft Lists is a powerful tool that can transform how you manage and organize information. Its flexibility, integration capabilities, and user-friendly design make it an essential part of the Microsoft 365 suite. Whether you're managing projects, tracking assets, or planning events, Microsoft Lists provides the tools you need to stay organized and productive.

As you delve deeper into this manual, you'll learn how to harness the full potential of Microsoft Lists, from basic setup to advanced features. The following chapters will guide you through each aspect of the application, providing practical examples and best practices to help you master Microsoft Lists and enhance your organizational capabilities.

In summary, Microsoft Lists is more than just a digital tool; it's a gateway to improved efficiency and collaboration. By leveraging its features, you can streamline your workflows, ensure data accuracy, and foster a more organized and productive work environment. Welcome to the world of Microsoft Lists, where organization meets innovation.

1.3 How to Use This Manual

The purpose of this manual is to serve as a comprehensive guide for users of all levels to effectively navigate and utilize Microsoft Lists. Whether you are a beginner just getting started or an advanced user looking to deepen your understanding, this manual is structured to meet your needs. The following sections will outline how you can best use this manual to maximize your efficiency and organization with Microsoft Lists.

Understanding the Structure of This Manual

This manual is divided into several chapters, each focusing on a specific aspect of Microsoft Lists. Here's a brief overview of the structure:

1. Introduction: This section provides an overview of the importance of organization, an introduction to Microsoft Lists, and instructions on how to use this manual.

2. Getting Started with Microsoft Lists: This chapter covers the basics, including an introduction to Microsoft Lists, setting up your Microsoft account, and navigating the interface.

3. Creating and Managing Lists: Here, you will learn how to create new lists, customize list columns, and use list views effectively.

4. Advanced List Features: This chapter delves into more advanced features such as integration with other Microsoft 365 apps, setting up alerts and notifications, and using rules and automations.

5. Collaborating with Microsoft Lists: Learn how to share lists with others, add comments, and track changes.

6. Managing Data in Microsoft Lists: This chapter covers importing and exporting data, data validation, and using calculated columns.

7. Visualizing Data with Microsoft Lists: Understand how to create charts and graphs, use conditional formatting, and set up calendar and gallery views.

8. Best Practices for Microsoft Lists: This chapter provides tips on organizing lists effectively, maintaining data integrity, and efficient workflow strategies.

9. Troubleshooting and Support: Find solutions to common issues, access support, and keep up with updates.

10. Conclusion: A summary of key points and encouragement for continued learning.

11. Appendices: Additional resources including templates, a glossary of terms, and references.

Navigating the Manual

To make the most of this manual, it is recommended to follow these navigation tips:

- Start with the Introduction: If you are new to Microsoft Lists, begin with the introduction to understand the importance of organization and what Microsoft Lists can do for you.

- Follow the Chapters Sequentially: For beginners, it's beneficial to read through the chapters in order. This will help you build a solid foundation before moving on to more advanced topics.

- Refer to Specific Sections as Needed: If you have specific questions or need to learn about a particular feature, use the table of contents to navigate directly to that section.

- Use the Appendices for Additional Resources: The appendices contain templates, a glossary of terms, and additional resources that can be very helpful as you work with Microsoft Lists.

Key Icons and Formatting

Throughout this manual, you will notice the use of various icons and formatting styles to highlight important information. Understanding these can help you quickly identify key points and navigate the content more efficiently.

- Tips and Tricks: Look for the light bulb icon for helpful tips and tricks that can enhance your use of Microsoft Lists.

- Important Notes: The exclamation mark icon is used to indicate important notes that you should pay attention to.

- Warnings: A warning triangle icon highlights potential pitfalls or common mistakes to avoid.

- Step-by-Step Instructions: Numbered lists provide clear, step-by-step instructions for performing tasks.

- Examples: Example sections are provided to illustrate how to apply concepts in real-world scenarios.

- Glossary Terms: Terms that are defined in the glossary are italicized on their first use.

Using This Manual for Self-Paced Learning

This manual is designed to accommodate self-paced learning. Whether you prefer to read through it quickly to get a broad understanding or take your time to master each section thoroughly, this manual supports both approaches.

- Quick Overview: If you are looking for a quick overview, focus on the introduction and the summary sections at the end of each chapter. These provide a concise explanation of the key points.

- Deep Dive: For a more in-depth understanding, take the time to work through the examples and practice the step-by-step instructions provided in each chapter. This hands-on approach will reinforce your learning and help you become proficient in using Microsoft Lists.

Customizing Your Learning Experience

Everyone's learning needs and preferences are different. This manual allows you to customize your learning experience based on your specific requirements.

- Identify Your Learning Goals: Before you start, take a moment to identify what you hope to achieve by using Microsoft Lists. Are you looking to manage personal projects more effectively, improve team collaboration, or streamline data management processes? Knowing your goals can help you focus on the most relevant sections of the manual.

- Adjust the Pace: Depending on your familiarity with similar tools, you may find some sections more intuitive than others. Feel free to adjust the pace at which you go through the chapters. Spend more time on sections that are new to you and quickly review those you are already comfortable with.

- Utilize Practice Exercises: Throughout the manual, you will find practice exercises that encourage you to apply what you have learned. These exercises are designed to reinforce your understanding and help you become more confident in using Microsoft Lists.

- Take Notes: As you read through the manual, take notes on key points and concepts. This will help you retain the information and serve as a quick reference in the future.

Leveraging Microsoft Lists in Different Scenarios

Microsoft Lists is a versatile tool that can be used in a variety of scenarios. This manual includes examples and case studies to help you understand how to apply Microsoft Lists in different contexts.

- Personal Organization: Learn how to use Microsoft Lists to manage personal tasks, track goals, and organize personal projects.

- Team Collaboration: Discover how to use Microsoft Lists to collaborate with team members, manage group projects, and streamline communication.

- Business Processes: Explore how Microsoft Lists can be used to manage business processes such as inventory tracking, customer relationship management, and project management.

Integrating with Other Tools

Microsoft Lists is part of the Microsoft 365 suite, which means it integrates seamlessly with other Microsoft applications. This manual will guide you on how to leverage these integrations to enhance your productivity.

- Microsoft Teams: Learn how to integrate Microsoft Lists with Microsoft Teams for better collaboration and communication within your team.

- Power Automate: Discover how to use Power Automate to create automated workflows that save time and reduce manual effort.

- Power BI: Understand how to connect Microsoft Lists with Power BI to visualize your data and gain valuable insights.

Staying Up-to-Date with Microsoft Lists

Microsoft continuously updates and improves its products, including Microsoft Lists. This manual provides tips on how to stay informed about the latest updates and features.

- Microsoft Documentation: Regularly check the official Microsoft documentation for the latest information on Microsoft Lists.

- Community Forums: Join community forums and discussion groups to learn from other users and share your experiences.

- Webinars and Training Sessions: Participate in webinars and training sessions offered by Microsoft to stay current with new features and best practices.

Accessing Support

Even with a comprehensive manual, you may encounter questions or issues that require additional assistance. This manual includes information on how to access support resources.

- Help Center: Use the built-in help center in Microsoft Lists for quick answers to common questions.

- Support Tickets: Learn how to submit support tickets to Microsoft for more complex issues.

- Community Support: Join the Microsoft Lists community to ask questions and get help from other users.

Conclusion

This manual is designed to be your go-to resource for mastering Microsoft Lists. By following the chapters sequentially, referring to specific sections as needed, and leveraging the tips and examples provided, you will be well-equipped to organize your data and workflows effectively.

Whether you are a beginner just starting out or an advanced user looking to enhance your skills, this manual has something to offer. Use it as a reference guide, a learning tool, and a source of inspiration as you explore the many capabilities of Microsoft Lists

CHAPTER I
Getting Started with Microsoft Lists

1.1 Introduction to Microsoft Lists

Overview of Microsoft Lists

Microsoft Lists is a versatile and powerful application designed to help users track information, organize work, and manage data efficiently. As a part of the Microsoft 365 suite, it integrates seamlessly with other Microsoft apps, making it a vital tool for businesses, teams, and individuals aiming to streamline their workflow and enhance productivity. This section will delve into the core aspects of Microsoft Lists, including its purpose, features, and how it fits into the broader Microsoft ecosystem.

Purpose and Utility

At its core, Microsoft Lists is a modern information tracking app. Whether you're managing a project, tracking assets, or creating an event itinerary, Lists provides a flexible way to organize information. Its primary purpose is to offer a structured and customizable way to handle data, allowing users to create, share, and track lists that can range from simple task lists to complex project management dashboards.

Integration with Microsoft 365

One of the standout features of Microsoft Lists is its seamless integration with the Microsoft 365 ecosystem. This integration means that Lists can work in tandem with applications like Microsoft Teams, SharePoint, Outlook, and Power Automate. For instance, a list created in Microsoft Lists can be shared in a Teams channel, allowing team members to collaborate in real-time. This level of integration ensures that Lists is not just a standalone tool but a part of a cohesive productivity suite that enhances collaboration and efficiency.

Key Features

Microsoft Lists is packed with features designed to make data management straightforward and effective. Here are some of the key features that set it apart:

1. Templates: Microsoft Lists offers a variety of templates to help users get started quickly. These templates cover a wide range of use cases, such as event planning, issue tracking, asset management, and more. Each template is designed to be customizable, allowing users to tailor it to their specific needs.

2. Customizable Columns and Views: Users can add columns of various data types, such as text, number, choice, date, and more. This flexibility ensures that the lists can accommodate different kinds of information. Additionally, users can create custom views to display data in ways that best suit their requirements, such as grid, calendar, and gallery views.

3. Integration with Power Automate: Power Automate integration allows users to automate workflows directly from their lists. This feature can save time by automating repetitive tasks, such as sending notifications when a list item is updated or creating tasks in Planner based on list entries.

4. Conditional Formatting: This feature enables users to highlight list items that meet certain criteria. For example, tasks that are overdue can be displayed in red, or high-

priority issues can be bolded. Conditional formatting makes it easier to identify critical information at a glance.

5. Rich Text Editor: The rich text editor allows users to format text within list items, making the information more readable and visually appealing. Users can add links, images, and tables, enhancing the overall functionality of the lists.

6. Mobile Access: Microsoft Lists is accessible via mobile apps for iOS and Android, ensuring that users can manage their lists on the go. The mobile app offers most of the features available on the desktop version, providing flexibility and convenience.

User Interface

The user interface of Microsoft Lists is designed to be intuitive and user-friendly. The main dashboard provides quick access to recent lists, favorites, and templates. Creating a new list is straightforward, with a guided process that walks users through selecting a template or starting from scratch. The interface also supports drag-and-drop functionality, making it easy to rearrange columns and list items.

Security and Compliance

As part of the Microsoft 365 suite, Microsoft Lists benefits from the robust security and compliance features offered by Microsoft. Data in Lists is encrypted both at rest and in transit, ensuring that sensitive information is protected. Additionally, Lists complies with major industry standards and regulations, such as GDPR, HIPAA, and ISO/IEC 27001. This compliance ensures that businesses can use Lists for critical operations without worrying about data security and regulatory adherence.

Collaborative Features

Microsoft Lists excels in collaborative environments. Users can share lists with colleagues, assign tasks, and comment on list items. Real-time collaboration is facilitated through integration with Microsoft Teams, where lists can be added as tabs within channels. This integration allows team members to discuss list items, make updates, and track progress without leaving the Teams environment. Furthermore, version history and activity tracking ensure that changes are transparent and accountable.

Customization and Extensibility

One of the strengths of Microsoft Lists is its customization capabilities. Users can create custom columns to capture specific types of data, such as person, currency, or calculated values. Additionally, developers can extend Lists functionality using the Microsoft Graph API, allowing for the creation of custom applications and integrations. This extensibility makes Microsoft Lists a versatile tool that can be adapted to meet the unique needs of any organization.

Use Cases

The versatility of Microsoft Lists makes it suitable for a wide range of use cases:

1. Project Management: Teams can use Lists to track project tasks, deadlines, and milestones. Custom views and conditional formatting can help highlight critical tasks and track progress.

2. Asset Management: Organizations can maintain a list of assets, including details such as purchase date, warranty information, and current status. This information can be easily accessed and updated by relevant team members.

3. Event Planning: Lists can be used to manage event details, such as schedules, guest lists, and vendor contacts. The calendar view is particularly useful for visualizing event timelines.

4. Issue Tracking: Support teams can use Lists to track customer issues, assign them to team members, and monitor their resolution status. Automated workflows can be set up to notify team members of new issues or status changes.

5. Employee Onboarding: HR departments can use Lists to manage the onboarding process for new employees, including task assignments, document tracking, and training schedules.

Conclusion

Microsoft Lists is a powerful and flexible tool that can significantly enhance the way organizations manage and track information. Its integration with the Microsoft 365 ecosystem, combined with its rich feature set and user-friendly interface, makes it an essential application for businesses of all sizes. Whether you are managing projects, tracking assets, or organizing events, Microsoft Lists provides the tools needed to stay organized and productive. By understanding the core features and benefits of Microsoft Lists, users can leverage its full potential to streamline their workflows and improve their data management processes.

Key Features and Benefits

Microsoft Lists is a powerful tool within the Microsoft 365 suite designed to help individuals and organizations manage information and track processes efficiently. In this section, we will explore the key features of Microsoft Lists and the benefits it offers to users.

Key Features of Microsoft Lists

1. Customizable Templates:

  - Ready-Made Templates: Microsoft Lists comes with a variety of templates that cater to different needs, such as event itineraries, asset tracking, issue tracking, and more. These templates provide a quick start, allowing users to leverage pre-configured structures and save time on setup.

  - Custom Templates: Users can create custom templates tailored to specific requirements. This feature is particularly useful for organizations with unique workflows, enabling them to standardize processes across teams and projects.

2. Column Types and Customization:

  - Rich Column Types: Microsoft Lists supports various column types, including text, number, choice, date and time, person, hyperlink, and more. Each column type serves different purposes, allowing users to capture diverse data accurately.

  - Custom Columns: Users can create custom columns to suit specific needs. For example, a custom column for project status with predefined choices such as "Not Started," "In Progress," and "Completed."

3. Views and Filtering:

- Multiple Views: Lists can be displayed in various views, such as grid view, calendar view, and gallery view. This flexibility allows users to visualize data in ways that are most meaningful to them.

- Advanced Filtering: Users can apply filters to narrow down the data displayed in a list. Advanced filtering options enable complex queries, helping users focus on the most relevant information.

4. Conditional Formatting:

- Visual Highlights: Conditional formatting allows users to apply custom formatting rules to list items based on specific criteria. For instance, tasks that are overdue can be highlighted in red, making it easy to identify critical issues at a glance.

5. Integration with Microsoft 365 Apps:

- Teams Integration: Microsoft Lists seamlessly integrates with Microsoft Teams, allowing users to access and manage their lists directly within the Teams interface. This integration fosters collaboration and ensures that list data is readily available during team discussions.

- Power Automate Integration: Lists can be connected to Power Automate to automate workflows. For example, users can set up automatic notifications when a list item is updated or create a task in Planner based on a list entry.

6. Collaboration and Sharing:

- Real-Time Collaboration: Multiple users can work on a list simultaneously, with real-time updates ensuring that everyone has access to the most current information.

- Sharing Options: Lists can be shared with individuals or groups within an organization. Users can set permissions to control who can view or edit the list, ensuring data security and integrity.

7. Mobile Access:

- Mobile App: Microsoft Lists is available as a mobile app for iOS and Android devices. The app provides a consistent experience across devices, allowing users to manage their lists on the go.

8. Integration with Microsoft Graph:

- Data Integration: Developers can use Microsoft Graph to integrate Lists data with other applications and services. This feature enables advanced scenarios, such as creating custom reports or dashboards that pull data from multiple sources.

Benefits of Using Microsoft Lists

1. Enhanced Organization:

- Centralized Data Management: Microsoft Lists provides a centralized platform for managing information. By consolidating data in one place, users can easily access, update, and track information, reducing the risk of data fragmentation and loss.

- Structured Data: The use of columns and templates ensures that data is captured in a structured format. This organization makes it easier to search, filter, and analyze information, leading to better decision-making.

2. Improved Collaboration:

- Team Collaboration: Real-time collaboration features allow team members to work together on lists, enhancing communication and productivity. Shared lists ensure that everyone is on the same page, reducing miscommunication and duplication of effort.

- Comments and Mentions: Users can add comments to list items and mention colleagues to draw their attention to specific entries. This feature facilitates discussion and ensures that important information is not overlooked.

3. Increased Efficiency:

- Automation: Integration with Power Automate allows users to automate repetitive tasks, saving time and reducing the likelihood of errors. Automated workflows can handle tasks such as sending notifications, updating status, or creating related records, freeing up users to focus on more strategic activities.

- Templates and Customization: Ready-made templates and the ability to create custom templates accelerate the setup process. Users can quickly get started with predefined structures and then customize them to fit their specific needs, improving efficiency and reducing setup time.

4. Better Data Visualization:

   - Custom Views: Multiple view options allow users to visualize data in different ways, making it easier to understand and analyze information. For example, calendar views are ideal for tracking events and deadlines, while gallery views provide a visually appealing way to display images and media.

   - Conditional Formatting: By applying conditional formatting rules, users can highlight important data points, making it easier to identify trends, outliers, and critical information.

5. Scalability and Flexibility:

   - Adaptable to Various Use Cases: Microsoft Lists is highly adaptable and can be used for a wide range of applications, from simple task tracking to complex project management. Its flexibility ensures that it can scale to meet the needs of both small teams and large organizations.

   - Integration with Other Tools: The ability to integrate with other Microsoft 365 apps and third-party services ensures that Lists can fit seamlessly into existing workflows. This interoperability allows users to leverage their existing tools and data, enhancing overall efficiency.

6. Data Security and Compliance:

   - Access Controls: Robust permission settings allow users to control who can view or edit list data. This feature ensures that sensitive information is protected and only accessible to authorized individuals.

   - Compliance: Microsoft Lists adheres to industry standards and regulations for data security and compliance. Organizations can be confident that their data is stored securely and managed in accordance with best practices.

7. User-Friendly Interface:

   - Intuitive Design: The user-friendly interface of Microsoft Lists makes it accessible to users of all skill levels. The clean, intuitive design ensures that users can quickly learn how to navigate and use the tool effectively.

   - Consistency Across Devices: The consistent experience across web and mobile platforms ensures that users can access and manage their lists from anywhere, at any time. This flexibility supports remote work and on-the-go access.

8. Support and Community:

- Microsoft Support: Users have access to extensive support resources, including documentation, tutorials, and community forums. Microsoft provides regular updates and improvements to the Lists app, ensuring that users benefit from the latest features and enhancements.

- Community Engagement: The active Microsoft Lists community provides a platform for users to share tips, best practices, and solutions. Engaging with the community can help users maximize the value of Microsoft Lists and stay informed about new developments.

Conclusion

Microsoft Lists offers a robust set of features designed to help users organize, manage, and track information efficiently. Its customizable templates, rich column types, and multiple view options provide the flexibility needed to handle a variety of use cases. Integration with other Microsoft 365 apps and automation tools further enhances its capabilities, making it a powerful tool for improving collaboration, efficiency, and data visualization.

By leveraging the key features and benefits of Microsoft Lists, users can enhance their organizational workflows, streamline processes, and make more informed decisions. Whether you are managing a simple task list or a complex project, Microsoft Lists provides the tools you need to stay organized and productive.

As we continue through this guide, we will delve deeper into the specifics of setting up and using Microsoft Lists, exploring advanced features and best practices to help you master this powerful tool.

1.2 Setting Up Your Microsoft Account

To fully utilize Microsoft Lists, you need to have a Microsoft account. A Microsoft account not only grants you access to Microsoft Lists but also integrates seamlessly with other Microsoft 365 applications, enhancing your productivity and enabling collaborative efforts. In this section, we will guide you through the process of creating a Microsoft account, ensuring you are set up and ready to start organizing with Microsoft Lists.

Creating a Microsoft Account

Why You Need a Microsoft Account

Before we dive into the steps of creating a Microsoft account, it's important to understand why having one is essential:

1. Access to Microsoft Services: A Microsoft account provides access to a wide range of services including Microsoft Lists, Outlook, OneDrive, and more.

2. Seamless Integration: It allows for seamless integration with Microsoft 365 apps, enhancing productivity and collaboration.

3. Data Synchronization: Your data is synchronized across devices, ensuring you have access to your lists and documents wherever you are.

4. Security and Support: Microsoft accounts come with robust security features and customer support options, ensuring your data is protected and help is available when needed.

Step-by-Step Guide to Creating a Microsoft Account

Step 1: Visit the Microsoft Account Sign-Up Page

To begin, open your preferred web browser and navigate to the Microsoft account sign-up page. You can do this by typing "Microsoft account sign up" into your search engine or by directly visiting https://signup.live.com.

Step 2: Start the Sign-Up Process

On the sign-up page, you will see options to sign in if you already have an account or to create a new one. Click on the "Create account" link to start the process of creating a new Microsoft account.

Step 3: Choose Your Account Type

Microsoft allows you to create an account using either an existing email address or a new Outlook email address. If you already have an email address you'd like to use, you can choose the "Use your email address" option. If you prefer a new Outlook email address, select the "Get a new email address" option.

- Using an Existing Email Address: Enter your existing email address in the provided field and click "Next".

- Creating a New Outlook Email Address: Click on the "Get a new email address" option, then enter your desired email address and choose between @outlook.com and @hotmail.com.

Step 4: Create a Password

Next, you'll be prompted to create a password for your Microsoft account. Your password should be strong, combining letters, numbers, and special characters to ensure the security of your account. Enter your chosen password and click "Next".

Step 5: Enter Your Personal Information

Microsoft will ask for some basic personal information to set up your account. This includes your first name, last name, country/region, and birthdate. Fill in the required fields and click "Next".

Step 6: Verify Your Email Address

To verify your email address, Microsoft will send a verification code to the email address you provided. Check your email inbox for a message from Microsoft, then enter the verification code in the appropriate field on the sign-up page and click "Next".

Step 7: Solve the CAPTCHA

As a security measure, Microsoft may ask you to solve a CAPTCHA to ensure you are not a bot. Follow the on-screen instructions to complete the CAPTCHA challenge, then click "Next".

Step 8: Agree to the Terms of Service and Privacy Policy

Read through Microsoft's Terms of Service and Privacy Policy. Once you've reviewed the terms, check the box indicating your agreement, then click "Next" to finalize the creation of your Microsoft account.

Step 9: Set Up Account Recovery Options

To secure your account and make it easier to recover in case you forget your password, Microsoft will prompt you to set up account recovery options. You can provide a phone number or an alternative email address for recovery purposes. Follow the on-screen instructions to add these recovery options.

Step 10: Customize Your Account Settings

After setting up your account recovery options, you'll have the opportunity to customize some of your account settings. This includes language preferences, time zone, and other personalization options. Adjust these settings according to your preferences and click "Next".

Step 11: Accessing Microsoft Lists

Once your Microsoft account is created, you can access Microsoft Lists by signing in to your Microsoft account on the Microsoft 365 homepage. Navigate to https://www.office.com and sign in with your new Microsoft account credentials. From the Microsoft 365 dashboard, you can access Microsoft Lists along with other Microsoft 365 applications.

Tips for Managing Your Microsoft Account

- Keep Your Password Secure: Ensure your password is unique and not easily guessable. Avoid using common words or phrases and update your password regularly.

- Enable Two-Factor Authentication (2FA): Enhance the security of your Microsoft account by enabling two-factor authentication. This adds an extra layer of security by requiring a second form of verification in addition to your password.

- Update Your Recovery Options: Regularly review and update your account recovery options to ensure they are current. This will make it easier to recover your account if you ever forget your password.

- Monitor Account Activity: Periodically check your account activity for any unusual or unauthorized actions. If you notice any suspicious activity, report it to Microsoft and change your password immediately.

Conclusion

Creating a Microsoft account is a straightforward process that unlocks a multitude of features and services, including Microsoft Lists. By following the steps outlined in this section, you can set up your account with ease and begin organizing your data efficiently. With a secure and well-managed Microsoft account, you'll be well-equipped to leverage the full potential of Microsoft Lists and other Microsoft 365 applications.

Accessing Microsoft Lists

Accessing Microsoft Lists is a straightforward process that involves a few essential steps. Whether you are a first-time user or transitioning from another data management tool, understanding how to access Microsoft Lists efficiently is crucial for maximizing its potential. In this section, we will cover the various methods to access Microsoft Lists, prerequisites, and common troubleshooting tips.

1. Understanding the Prerequisites

Before accessing Microsoft Lists, it is important to ensure that you meet the necessary prerequisites. These include:

1. A Microsoft 365 Subscription: Microsoft Lists is part of the Microsoft 365 suite. Therefore, you need an active subscription to Microsoft 365, which can be either a personal, business, or enterprise plan. Ensure that your subscription includes access to Microsoft Lists.

2. Internet Connection: Since Microsoft Lists is a cloud-based service, a stable internet connection is required to access and manage your lists.

3. Supported Browser or App: Microsoft Lists can be accessed through a web browser or via the Microsoft Lists mobile app. Ensure you are using a supported browser such as Microsoft Edge, Google Chrome, Safari, or Firefox. For mobile access, the Microsoft Lists app is available for both iOS and Android devices.

2. Accessing Microsoft Lists via Web Browser

Accessing Microsoft Lists through a web browser is one of the most common methods. Follow these steps to get started:

1. Sign In to Microsoft 365:

   - Open your preferred web browser and navigate to the Microsoft 365 homepage (https://www.office.com).

   - Click on the "Sign In" button located at the top right corner of the page.

   - Enter your Microsoft 365 credentials (email and password) and click "Sign In."

2. Navigating to Microsoft Lists:

   - Once you are signed in, you will be directed to the Microsoft 365 dashboard. Here, you can see all the apps available in your subscription.

- Look for the "Lists" icon. If you do not see it immediately, click on the "All Apps" link to view the complete list of Microsoft 365 applications.

- Click on the "Lists" icon to open Microsoft Lists.

3. Creating a Shortcut for Easy Access:

- For quicker access in the future, you can bookmark the Microsoft Lists URL (https://lists.microsoft.com) in your browser.

- Alternatively, you can pin the Lists app to your Microsoft 365 app launcher for easy access from the dashboard.

3. Accessing Microsoft Lists via Microsoft Teams

Microsoft Teams integrates seamlessly with Microsoft Lists, allowing you to access and manage your lists directly within the Teams environment. This is particularly useful for collaborative projects and team-based workflows. Follow these steps to access Microsoft Lists via Teams:

1. Open Microsoft Teams:

- Launch the Microsoft Teams application on your desktop or open the Teams web app (https://teams.microsoft.com).

- Sign in with your Microsoft 365 credentials if prompted.

2. Navigating to Lists in Teams:

- In the Teams interface, select the "Teams" tab from the sidebar.

- Choose the team and channel where you want to add or access a list.

- Click on the "+" icon at the top of the channel to add a new tab.

- From the list of available apps, select "Lists" and click "Save."

3. Creating or Accessing Lists:

- Once the Lists tab is added to your channel, you can create a new list or access existing ones.

- Use the interface to manage your lists, add new items, and collaborate with team members in real-time.

4. Accessing Microsoft Lists via Mobile App

For on-the-go access, the Microsoft Lists mobile app provides a user-friendly interface to manage your lists from your smartphone or tablet. Follow these steps to access Microsoft Lists via the mobile app:

1. Download the App:

   - Visit the App Store (iOS) or Google Play Store (Android) on your mobile device.

   - Search for "Microsoft Lists" and download the app.

2. Sign In:

   - Open the Microsoft Lists app and sign in with your Microsoft 365 credentials.

3. Using the Mobile Interface:

   - The mobile app provides a streamlined interface for creating and managing lists.

   - You can create new lists, add items, and view list details with ease.

   - Use the app's features to stay organized and keep track of tasks, even when you are away from your desk.

5. Common Troubleshooting Tips

While accessing Microsoft Lists is generally straightforward, you might encounter some issues. Here are common troubleshooting tips to help you resolve any problems:

1. Sign-In Issues:

   - Ensure that you are using the correct Microsoft 365 credentials.

   - If you have forgotten your password, use the "Forgot Password" link to reset it.

2. Browser Compatibility:

   - Make sure you are using a supported browser.

   - Clear your browser cache and cookies if you experience loading issues.

3. App Performance:

- Ensure that your mobile app is up to date by checking for updates in the App Store or Google Play Store.

- Restart the app or your device if you encounter performance issues.

4. Network Connectivity:

  - Verify that you have a stable internet connection.

  - Switch to a different network if you experience connectivity problems.

6. Enhancing Your Access Experience

To make the most out of Microsoft Lists, consider the following tips to enhance your access experience:

1. Customize Your Dashboard:

  - Personalize your Microsoft 365 dashboard by rearranging the apps and creating shortcuts to frequently used tools, including Microsoft Lists.

2. Use Keyboard Shortcuts:

  - Familiarize yourself with keyboard shortcuts to navigate Microsoft Lists more efficiently. For example, pressing "Ctrl + /" will display a list of available shortcuts.

3. Enable Notifications:

  - Configure notifications to stay updated on changes to your lists. This can be done through the settings menu in both the web and mobile apps.

4. Leverage Integrations:

  - Take advantage of integrations with other Microsoft 365 apps such as Outlook, Planner, and Power Automate to streamline your workflows and enhance productivity.

7. Conclusion

Accessing Microsoft Lists is a simple yet essential process that forms the foundation of effective list management. By understanding the various methods to access Microsoft Lists and implementing the tips provided, you can ensure a seamless and productive experience. Whether you are using the web browser, integrating with Teams, or managing lists on your mobile device, Microsoft Lists offers the flexibility and functionality needed to stay organized and efficient.

1.3 Navigating the Interface

Main Dashboard

The Main Dashboard is the central hub of Microsoft Lists, where users can create, manage, and interact with their lists. Understanding how to navigate the Main Dashboard is essential for efficiently using Microsoft Lists. This section will provide a comprehensive guide to the Main Dashboard, covering its layout, functionalities, and tips for optimizing your experience.

1. Understanding the Layout

The Main Dashboard of Microsoft Lists is designed to be user-friendly and intuitive, allowing users to access and manage their lists with ease. The layout consists of several key components:

- Header Bar: The header bar runs across the top of the dashboard and contains the Microsoft Lists logo, search bar, and user account information. This area provides quick access to account settings and notifications.

- Navigation Pane: Located on the left side, the navigation pane includes links to your recent lists, favorite lists, and various templates. It also provides quick access to creating new lists.

- Main Workspace: The central area of the dashboard where lists are displayed and interacted with. This workspace is dynamic, changing based on the selected list or action.

- Command Bar: Situated just above the main workspace, the command bar contains tools and options for managing lists, such as creating new items, filtering, and exporting data.

2. Using the Header Bar

The header bar is a critical component for overall navigation and accessing essential features:

- Search Bar: The search bar allows users to quickly find specific lists or items within lists. Enter keywords related to the list or item you're looking for, and the search function will provide relevant results.

- User Account Information: Clicking on your profile picture or initials in the header bar will open a menu with options for accessing your account settings, managing notifications, and signing out. This area also provides shortcuts to other Microsoft 365 apps.

3. Exploring the Navigation Pane

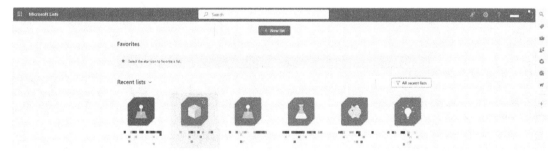

The navigation pane is your gateway to accessing and managing lists. It includes several sections:

- Recent: Displays lists you have recently accessed, allowing for quick navigation back to them.

 - Favorites: Lists you have marked as favorites for easy access. To favorite a list, simply click the star icon next to its name.

- All Lists: A complete list of all the lists you have access to. This section is categorized to help you find lists based on different criteria.

- Templates: Provides access to a variety of pre-built templates that you can use to create new lists quickly. Templates are categorized by use cases such as project management, event planning, and issue tracking.

4. Interacting with the Main Workspace

The main workspace is where the magic happens. It's the area where you will spend most of your time interacting with your lists. Here are some of the key features:

- List Display: The primary function of the main workspace is to display the contents of the selected list. You can view items in various formats, such as grid view, list view, or gallery view, depending on your preference and the nature of your data.

- Adding and Managing Items: The main workspace provides tools for adding new items to your lists, editing existing items, and managing list settings. You can add new items using the 'New' button in the command bar or by using keyboard shortcuts.

- Sorting and Filtering: Use the options in the command bar to sort and filter the items in your list. This helps in organizing data and finding specific items quickly. You can sort items based on different columns or apply filters to narrow down the displayed items based on specific criteria.

5. Utilizing the Command Bar

The command bar is packed with tools and options for managing your lists. Here are some of the primary features:

- New Item: Create a new item in the selected list by clicking the 'New' button. This opens a form where you can enter details for the new item.

- Edit: Select an item in the list and click 'Edit' to modify its details. The edit form allows you to change any information stored in the item's columns.

- Filter: Apply filters to your list to view only the items that meet specific criteria. Filters can be based on column values, date ranges, or custom conditions.

- Export: Export the list data to other formats, such as Excel or CSV. This is useful for offline analysis or sharing data with others who do not have access to Microsoft Lists.

6. Tips for Optimizing Your Experience

To make the most out of the Main Dashboard, consider the following tips:

- Customize Your Views: Create custom views that display data in a way that suits your needs. You can save these views and switch between them as needed.

- Use Keyboard Shortcuts: Microsoft Lists supports various keyboard shortcuts that can speed up your workflow. Familiarize yourself with these shortcuts to enhance your efficiency.

- Leverage Templates: Don't start from scratch if you don't have to. Utilize the pre-built templates available in the navigation pane to quickly set up lists for common scenarios.

- Organize with Favorites: Mark frequently used lists as favorites to keep them easily accessible. This reduces the time spent searching for important lists.

- Stay Updated: Microsoft regularly updates Lists with new features and improvements. Keep an eye on the notification area in the header bar for announcements and updates.

Conclusion

Navigating the Main Dashboard in Microsoft Lists is straightforward once you understand its layout and functionalities. By leveraging the header bar, navigation pane, main workspace, and command bar, you can efficiently manage your lists and data. With these tools at your disposal, you're well on your way to mastering Microsoft Lists and optimizing your organizational workflows.

Creating Your First List

Creating your first list in Microsoft Lists is a fundamental step towards mastering the tool and leveraging its full potential. In this section, we'll guide you through each stage of creating a list, ensuring you understand the nuances and features available to tailor the list to your specific needs. Whether you're organizing a project, tracking issues, or managing inventory, this guide will help you set up your list effectively.

1. Understanding List Templates

Microsoft Lists offers a variety of templates to get you started quickly. Templates are pre-configured lists designed for specific use cases, such as issue tracking, event itineraries, and asset management. Each template comes with a predefined set of columns and views that you can customize further. When you begin creating your first list, choosing the right template can save time and provide a solid foundation.

2. Accessing the List Creation Wizard

To create a new list, start by navigating to the Microsoft Lists app. You can access it directly from the Microsoft 365 app launcher or by visiting the Lists home page within your SharePoint site. Once you're in the Lists app, click on the "New list" button to launch the list creation wizard.

3. Choosing a List Template

The list creation wizard presents several options for starting your list:

- Blank List: Start from scratch with a completely empty list.

- From Excel: Import data from an existing Excel spreadsheet.

- From Existing List: Use the structure of an existing list as a template.

- Templates: Choose from a variety of pre-designed templates.

For beginners, we recommend starting with a template that closely matches your intended use case. For example, if you're managing a project, the "Project Tasks" template can be an excellent starting point. Select your desired template and click "Use template" to proceed.

4. Naming Your List and Adding a Description

After selecting a template, you'll be prompted to name your list and provide a description. The name should be concise yet descriptive, making it easy to identify among your other lists. The description field allows you to explain the list's purpose, which can be helpful for other users who access the list.

Example:

- Name: Project Task Tracker

- Description: A list to track tasks, deadlines, and progress for the XYZ project.

5. Configuring List Columns

Once you've named your list, you'll move on to configuring the columns. Columns are the fields where your data is stored, and each template comes with a predefined set of columns tailored to its use case. You can add, remove, or modify columns to suit your needs.

- Adding Columns: Click on the "Add column" button to choose from a variety of column types, such as text, number, date, choice, and more. For instance, you might add a "Priority" column to your task tracker.

- Modifying Columns: Click on the column header and select "Column settings" to edit the properties of an existing column. You can change the column name, data type, and other settings.

- Removing Columns: If a template includes columns you don't need, you can remove them by selecting the column header and choosing "Remove."

6. Setting Up Column Formatting

Column formatting allows you to visually distinguish data based on specific criteria. For example, you can highlight high-priority tasks in red or overdue tasks in bold. To apply column formatting, click on the column header, select "Column settings," and then choose "Format this column." Microsoft Lists provides a straightforward interface for applying conditional formatting rules without needing to write code.

7. Creating Custom Views

Views control how the list data is displayed. The template may come with several predefined views, such as a grid view, calendar view, or board view. You can create custom views to focus on specific aspects of your data.

- Grid View: The default view, ideal for most data entry and review tasks.

- Calendar View: Useful for tracking tasks or events over time.

- Board View: Visualize tasks in a Kanban-style board, ideal for project management.

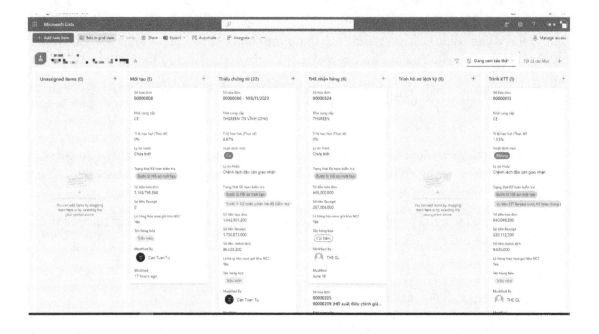

To create a custom view, click on the "View options" button and select "Create new view." Choose the view type and configure the settings to display the columns and data that are most relevant to your needs. For instance, you might create a view that only shows high-priority tasks or tasks assigned to a specific team member.

8. Saving and Sharing Your List

Once you've configured your list and views, it's time to save and share it with your team. Click the "Save" button to finalize the list setup. To share the list, click on the "Share" button at the top right corner. You can invite team members by entering their email addresses and selecting their permission levels (e.g., read, edit, or full control).

9. Adding and Managing List Items

With your list set up, you can start adding items. Each row in your list represents an item, such as a task, event, or asset. To add an item, click on the "New" button. Fill in the fields as required and click "Save." You can edit or delete items by selecting them and choosing the appropriate action from the toolbar.

10. Using Quick Edit for Bulk Data Entry

For faster data entry, use the "Quick Edit" mode, which allows you to edit multiple items in a spreadsheet-like grid. Click on the "Quick Edit" button to switch to this mode. You can then tab through fields and make changes rapidly. This is particularly useful for bulk data updates or when importing data from external sources.

11. Integrating with Other Microsoft 365 Tools

Microsoft Lists integrates seamlessly with other Microsoft 365 tools like Teams, SharePoint, and Power Automate. For example, you can add your list to a Teams channel to facilitate collaboration or create automated workflows with Power Automate to streamline repetitive tasks.

12. Best Practices for List Management

- Consistent Naming Conventions: Use consistent naming conventions for lists and columns to avoid confusion.

- Regular Reviews: Periodically review and clean up your lists to remove outdated or irrelevant items.

- Training and Support: Provide training and resources for team members to ensure everyone can use the lists effectively.

- Backup and Export: Regularly export your list data for backup purposes or further analysis in Excel.

Conclusion

Creating your first list in Microsoft Lists is a straightforward process that sets the stage for effective data management and collaboration. By understanding the features and customization options available, you can tailor your lists to meet the specific needs of your projects and teams. With practice, you'll find that Microsoft Lists becomes an invaluable tool in your productivity arsenal, helping you stay organized and on top of your tasks.

CHAPTER II
Creating and Managing Lists

2.1 Creating a New List

Templates and Custom Lists

Creating lists in Microsoft Lists can greatly enhance your organization and productivity by enabling you to manage and track various types of data. This section focuses on the process of creating new lists using templates and custom lists, which are foundational skills for mastering Microsoft Lists.

Understanding Templates

Microsoft Lists offers a variety of pre-built templates designed to help you get started quickly. These templates are tailored for specific use cases, making it easy to create lists that meet your needs without starting from scratch. Each template includes predefined columns and settings that align with common scenarios.

Available Templates

Here are some of the most commonly used templates in Microsoft Lists:

1. Issue Tracker: Ideal for tracking issues, bugs, or tickets. It includes columns for title, description, priority, status, assigned to, and due date.

2. Employee Onboarding: Helps manage the onboarding process for new employees. It includes columns for employee name, department, start date, checklist items, and status.

3. Event Itinerary: Useful for planning events and keeping track of schedules. It includes columns for event name, date, time, location, and description.

4. Asset Manager: Helps track and manage physical assets. It includes columns for asset name, type, assigned to, purchase date, and status.

5. Project Planner: Assists in project planning and tracking. It includes columns for task name, start date, due date, assigned to, priority, and status.

Creating a List from a Template

To create a new list using a template, follow these steps:

1. Access Microsoft Lists: Open Microsoft Lists from your Microsoft 365 app launcher or directly via the Lists app.

2. Create New List: Click on the "New list" button to start the process.

3. Select Template: You will be presented with various options. Choose "Templates" to view the available templates.

4. Choose a Template: Browse through the templates and select one that suits your needs. Click on the template to proceed.

5. Customize Template: Enter a name for your list, provide a description, and choose a color and icon to represent your list. You can also select a location to save the list (e.g., a specific SharePoint site).

6. Create List: Click the "Create" button to generate your new list based on the chosen template.

Once the list is created, you can start adding data to it immediately. The predefined columns will guide you on what information to enter, ensuring consistency and completeness.

Custom Lists

While templates are useful for many scenarios, there are times when you need to create a list that is tailored to your specific requirements. Custom lists allow you to define the structure and contents of your list from scratch, giving you complete control over the columns, data types, and settings.

Creating a Custom List

To create a custom list, follow these steps:

1. Access Microsoft Lists: Open Microsoft Lists from your Microsoft 365 app launcher or directly via the Lists app.

2. Create New List: Click on the "New list" button to start the process.

3. Select Blank List: Choose the "Blank list" option to create a list without any predefined structure.

4. Define List Properties: Enter a name for your list, provide a description, and choose a color and icon to represent your list. Select a location to save the list.

5. Create List: Click the "Create" button to generate your new blank list.

Adding Columns to a Custom List

With your custom list created, the next step is to add columns that define the structure and type of data you will be managing. Follow these steps to add and configure columns:

1. Add New Column: Click on the "Add column" button at the top of the list.

2. Choose Column Type: Select the type of column you want to add. Microsoft Lists offers a variety of column types, including:

  - Single line of text: For short text entries.

  - Multiple lines of text: For longer text entries.

  - Number: For numerical data.

  - Choice: For predefined options in a drop-down menu.

  - Date and time: For date and time entries.

  - Yes/No: For binary choices.

  - Person or group: For selecting users or groups.

  - Lookup: For referencing data from another list.

  - Hyperlink or picture: For URLs or images.

- Currency: For financial data.

3. Configure Column Settings: After selecting the column type, configure its settings. This typically involves providing a name for the column, specifying any additional options (e.g., default values, required fields), and setting up formatting rules if necessary.

4. Save Column: Click the "Save" button to add the column to your list.

Repeat these steps to add as many columns as needed to fully define the structure of your custom list.

Using Custom Columns

Once your columns are set up, you can start entering data into your custom list. The flexibility of custom lists allows you to capture exactly the information you need, organized in a way that makes sense for your specific use case.

Best Practices for Creating Lists

To ensure that your lists are effective and easy to use, consider the following best practices:

1. Plan Your List Structure: Before creating a list, take some time to plan its structure. Identify the types of data you need to capture and how they relate to each other. This will help you design a list that is both comprehensive and efficient.

2. Use Descriptive Column Names: Choose column names that clearly describe the data they will hold. This will make it easier for users to understand and use the list.

3. Leverage Choice Columns: When possible, use choice columns to provide predefined options for users. This helps maintain data consistency and makes data entry faster and more accurate.

4. Set Up Validation Rules: Use validation rules to enforce data integrity. For example, you can require that certain columns must be filled out, or that numerical entries fall within a specific range.

5. Utilize Views: Create custom views to display your data in different ways. This can help users find the information they need more quickly and easily.

6. Regularly Review and Update Lists: Periodically review your lists to ensure they remain relevant and useful. Update columns and views as needed to accommodate changing requirements.

Conclusion

Creating new lists in Microsoft Lists, whether using templates or custom structures, is a fundamental skill that can greatly enhance your ability to organize and manage data. Templates provide a quick and easy way to get started with predefined structures, while custom lists offer the flexibility to tailor the list to your specific needs. By following best practices and leveraging the powerful features of Microsoft Lists, you can create efficient, effective lists that support your workflows and improve productivity.

Importing Data to Create Lists

In today's data-driven world, the ability to import data efficiently is crucial for maintaining productivity and ensuring accurate information management. Microsoft Lists provides a seamless way to import data from various sources, allowing users to quickly populate lists without manual entry. This section will guide you through the process of importing data to create lists, covering the sources from which you can import data, the steps involved, and best practices for ensuring a smooth import process.

Sources for Importing Data

Microsoft Lists supports importing data from multiple sources, making it a versatile tool for data management. Here are the primary sources you can use to import data into Microsoft Lists:

1. Excel Spreadsheets: Excel is one of the most common tools for data management, and Microsoft Lists allows you to import data directly from Excel files.

2. CSV Files: Comma-Separated Values (CSV) files are widely used for data exchange and can be easily imported into Microsoft Lists.

3. Existing SharePoint Lists: If you are already using SharePoint, you can import data from existing SharePoint lists.

4. Other Microsoft 365 Apps: You can also import data from other Microsoft 365 applications such as Microsoft Teams, Planner, and OneNote.

Steps to Import Data from Excel

Excel spreadsheets are a popular choice for managing data, and importing this data into Microsoft Lists is straightforward. Here's a step-by-step guide to importing data from an Excel spreadsheet:

1. Prepare Your Excel File: Before importing, ensure that your Excel file is properly formatted. Each column in your spreadsheet should have a header, and the data should be organized in rows. Avoid merging cells or using complex formulas in the data you plan to import.

2. Open Microsoft Lists: Navigate to the Microsoft Lists app from your Microsoft 365 home page or through the app launcher.

3. Create a New List: Click on the "New list" button on the main dashboard. You will be presented with several options for creating a list. Choose the "From Excel" option.

4. Upload Your Excel File: A dialog box will prompt you to upload your Excel file. Click on the "Upload file" button and select the Excel file you want to import.

5. Map Columns: After uploading the file, you will need to map the columns from your Excel spreadsheet to the columns in your new list. Microsoft Lists will automatically detect and suggest column types based on the data, but you can adjust these settings as needed. Ensure that each column is correctly mapped to ensure data accuracy.

6. Configure List Settings: Once the columns are mapped, you can configure additional settings for your list, such as naming the list, adding a description, and setting up permissions. Click "Create" to finalize the import process.

Importing Data from CSV Files

CSV files are another common format for data exchange. The process of importing data from a CSV file into Microsoft Lists is similar to importing from Excel:

1. Prepare Your CSV File: Ensure that your CSV file is properly formatted with headers for each column and data organized in rows. Avoid using special characters that could disrupt the import process.

2. Open Microsoft Lists: Go to the Microsoft Lists app.

3. Create a New List: Click on "New list" and choose the "From CSV" option.

4. Upload Your CSV File: Click "Upload file" and select your CSV file.

5. Map Columns: Map the columns from your CSV file to the columns in the new list. Review the suggested column types and make any necessary adjustments.

6. Configure List Settings: After mapping the columns, configure the list settings and click "Create" to complete the import.

Importing Data from Existing SharePoint Lists

If you are using SharePoint and have existing lists, you can import this data into Microsoft Lists to consolidate your data management:

1. Open Microsoft Lists: Access the Microsoft Lists app.

2. Create a New List: Click on "New list" and select the "From existing list" option.

3. Choose a SharePoint List: A dialog box will appear, allowing you to browse and select an existing SharePoint list from your sites.

4. Configure List Settings: After selecting the SharePoint list, you can configure additional settings for your new list in Microsoft Lists. Click "Create" to finalize the import.

Best Practices for Data Import

To ensure a smooth and successful data import process, consider the following best practices:

1. Data Cleaning: Before importing data, clean your source data by removing duplicates, correcting errors, and ensuring consistent formatting. This helps prevent issues during the import process and ensures accurate data in your lists.

2. Column Mapping: Carefully map the columns from your source data to the columns in Microsoft Lists. Ensure that each column is correctly identified and appropriately typed (e.g., text, number, date).

3. Validation: After importing data, validate the imported list by reviewing a sample of entries to ensure that the data has been correctly imported and that there are no discrepancies.

4. Backup: Always keep a backup of your source data before importing. This ensures that you can revert to the original data if any issues arise during the import process.

5. Test Imports: For large datasets, consider performing a test import with a smaller subset of data to identify any potential issues before importing the entire dataset.

6. Use Templates: If you frequently import similar types of data, consider creating templates in Microsoft Lists. Templates can save time by pre-configuring columns and settings, ensuring consistency across multiple lists.

Common Issues and Troubleshooting

While importing data into Microsoft Lists is generally straightforward, you may encounter some common issues. Here are a few troubleshooting tips:

1. File Format Issues: Ensure that your Excel or CSV file is correctly formatted. Incorrect formatting, such as missing headers or unsupported characters, can cause import failures.

2. Column Mapping Errors: Double-check your column mappings to ensure that each column is correctly identified and appropriately typed. Incorrect mappings can result in data being imported incorrectly or not at all.

3. Large Data Sets: For very large datasets, the import process may take longer or may encounter issues. Consider breaking large datasets into smaller chunks and importing them separately.

4. Permissions: Ensure that you have the necessary permissions to create and modify lists in Microsoft Lists. Insufficient permissions can prevent you from completing the import process.

5. Data Integrity: After importing data, review the imported list to ensure data integrity. Check for any missing or incorrectly imported data and make necessary adjustments.

Conclusion

Importing data into Microsoft Lists is a powerful feature that enhances its utility and flexibility for data management. By following the steps outlined in this section, you can efficiently import data from various sources, ensuring that your lists are populated with accurate and relevant information. Adhering to best practices and being mindful of common issues will help you navigate the import process smoothly, allowing you to leverage the full potential of Microsoft Lists for your organizational needs.

In the next section, we will explore how to customize list columns to further tailor your lists to meet specific requirements. Customizing columns allows you to add new fields, modify existing ones, and utilize various column types to best represent your data.

2.2 Customizing List Columns

Customizing list columns in Microsoft Lists is an essential aspect of tailoring your lists to meet specific needs. It allows users to define the data structure and format, ensuring that the information captured is relevant and useful. This section will guide you through the process of adding and modifying columns in Microsoft Lists, providing detailed steps, best practices, and practical examples to help you get the most out of this powerful feature.

Adding and Modifying Columns

Columns in Microsoft Lists serve as the building blocks of your data structure. They determine the type of data that can be entered and how it is displayed. Adding and modifying columns is straightforward, but understanding the different types of columns available and their properties is crucial for effective list management.

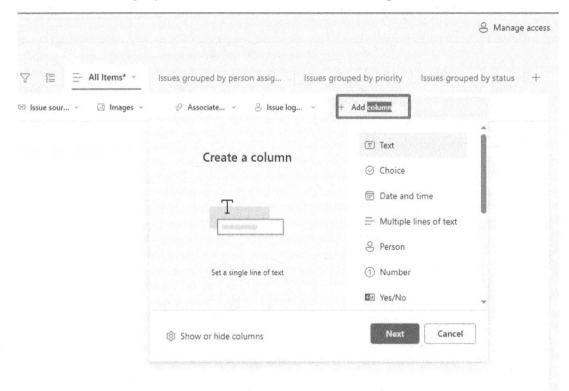

Adding Columns

1. Accessing the List Settings:

To add a column to your list, first navigate to the list you want to customize. Click on the "Add column" button located on the toolbar at the top of the list. This will open a dropdown menu with various column options.

2. Choosing a Column Type:

Microsoft Lists offers a variety of column types to suit different data requirements. The available column types include:

- Single line of text: Ideal for short text entries.

- Multiple lines of text: Suitable for longer text entries or notes.

- Number: Used for numerical data, with options for decimal places.

- Yes/No: A simple checkbox for binary choices.

- Choice: Allows you to create a dropdown list of predefined options.

- Date and Time: For capturing dates and times.

- Person or Group: To assign items to users or groups within your organization.

- Hyperlink: For adding URLs.

- Currency: Used for financial data, with currency formatting.

- Lookup: Links to data from another list.

- Calculated: Creates a column based on a formula.

- Managed Metadata: Uses terms from a managed metadata service.

- Location: For geographical data.

3. Defining Column Settings:

After selecting a column type, you will be prompted to define its settings. Common settings include:

- Column Name: A descriptive name for the column.

- Description: An optional field to explain the purpose of the column.

- Required Field: Determines whether the column must have a value.

- Default Value: Sets a default value for the column.

- Additional Settings: Depending on the column type, additional settings may be available, such as maximum character length for text columns or decimal places for number columns.

4. Saving the Column:

Once you have configured the column settings, click the "Save" button to add the column to your list. The new column will now be visible in the list view and ready for data entry.

Modifying Columns

1. Accessing Column Settings:

To modify an existing column, navigate to the list and click on the column header you wish to modify. From the dropdown menu, select "Column settings" and then "Edit."

2. Adjusting Column Properties:

You can change various properties of the column, such as the column name, description, and whether it is a required field. For some column types, additional properties can be modified. For example:

- Choice Columns: You can add or remove choices, change the display format (dropdown menu, radio buttons, or checkboxes), and set a default choice.

- Number Columns: You can adjust the number of decimal places, specify a minimum and maximum value, and set a default value.

- Date and Time Columns: You can choose to include the time along with the date and set a default date (current date, specific date, or no default).

3. Updating Data Validation:

Data validation rules ensure that the data entered into a column meets specific criteria. For example, in a number column, you can set rules to allow only positive numbers or numbers within a certain range. In a text column, you can limit the number of characters or specify a pattern that the text must match (using regular expressions).

4. Changing Column Order:

The order in which columns appear can be modified to enhance the readability and usability of your list. To change the column order, click on any column header, select "Column settings," and then "Move left" or "Move right" to reposition the column.

5. Deleting a Column:

If a column is no longer needed, it can be deleted. Click on the column header, select "Column settings," and then "Delete." Be cautious when deleting columns, as this action cannot be undone, and any data stored in the column will be lost.

Best Practices for Adding and Modifying Columns

1. Plan Your Columns:

Before adding columns, plan the structure of your list to ensure it meets your data capture and reporting needs. Consider the type of data you will be collecting and how it will be used.

2. Use Descriptive Names:

Use clear and descriptive names for your columns to make it easy for users to understand what data should be entered. Avoid using abbreviations or jargon that might be confusing.

3. Leverage Default Values:

Setting default values can save time and reduce errors during data entry. For example, if most entries will have the same status, set that status as the default value.

4. Implement Data Validation:

Use data validation rules to maintain data integrity. For example, if a column should only contain email addresses, use a regular expression to enforce this rule.

5. Keep It Simple:

Avoid adding too many columns, as this can make the list cumbersome to use. Focus on the essential data points and consider using additional lists or linked data sources for supplementary information.

Practical Examples

1. Creating a Project Management List:

Suppose you are creating a list to manage projects. The columns might include:

- Project Name (Single line of text)

- Project Manager (Person or Group)

- Start Date (Date and Time)

- End Date (Date and Time)

- Budget (Currency)

- Status (Choice: Not Started, In Progress, Completed)

- Notes (Multiple lines of text)

In this example, the "Status" column uses a choice field to standardize the project status entries. Default values can be set for the "Status" column to "Not Started" and for the "Budget" column to 0.

2. Creating an Inventory List:

For an inventory list, you might have columns such as:

- Item Name (Single line of text)

- Category (Choice: Electronics, Furniture, Stationery)

- Quantity (Number)

- Supplier (Lookup from Suppliers List)

- Purchase Date (Date and Time)

- Price (Currency)

- Location (Single line of text)

In this example, the "Supplier" column uses a lookup field to link data from another list, allowing for easy updates to supplier information without duplicating data.

3. Creating a Customer Feedback List:

A customer feedback list might include:

- Customer Name (Single line of text)

- Email (Single line of text)

- Feedback Date (Date and Time)

- Rating (Number: 1 to 5)

- Comments (Multiple lines of text)

- Resolved (Yes/No)

In this example, the "Rating" column uses a number field with validation to ensure ratings are between 1 and 5. The "Resolved" column uses a yes/no field to track whether the feedback has been addressed.

Conclusion

Adding and modifying columns in Microsoft Lists is a powerful way to customize your lists and ensure they meet your specific needs. By understanding the different column types and their properties, you can create lists that are both functional and user-friendly. Following best practices for column management will help maintain data integrity and improve the overall efficiency of your workflows. Whether you are managing projects, tracking inventory, or collecting feedback, Microsoft Lists offers the flexibility and features you need to stay organized and productive.

Column Types and Uses

Customizing list columns is a fundamental aspect of leveraging Microsoft Lists to its fullest potential. By understanding the various column types and their uses, you can tailor your lists to better suit your organizational needs, ensuring data is stored and displayed in the most effective manner possible.

Types of Columns

Microsoft Lists offers a variety of column types, each designed to hold different kinds of data. These columns can be categorized into several groups based on their functionality and the type of data they store:

1. Text Columns

2. Number Columns

3. Date and Time Columns

4. Choice Columns

5. Lookup Columns

6. Yes/No Columns

7. Person or Group Columns

8. Hyperlink Columns

9. Calculated Columns

10. Managed Metadata Columns

Let's explore each column type in detail, discussing their uses and benefits.

Text Columns

Single Line of Text:

- Description: This column type allows you to store a single line of text, suitable for short, straightforward data entries such as names, titles, or brief descriptions.

- Uses: Ideal for capturing brief information such as first names, job titles, or simple codes. For example, in a project tracking list, you might use this column to store task names.

Multiple Lines of Text:

- Description: This column type supports longer text entries and can include rich text formatting (such as bold, italics, and bullet points).

- Uses: Useful for storing detailed information like comments, notes, or long descriptions. In a customer feedback list, this column could capture detailed feedback from clients.

Number Columns

Number:

- Description: Stores numerical data, which can include integers or decimals. You can set a minimum and maximum value, as well as define decimal places.

- Uses: Suitable for any data that requires numerical values, such as quantities, prices, or scores. For instance, in a sales tracking list, this column could track the quantity of items sold.

Currency:

- Description: Specifically designed for monetary values, allowing you to select a currency format and define the number of decimal places.

- Uses: Essential for financial data, such as costs, revenues, or budgets. In a budgeting list, you might use this column to record the budgeted and actual costs of various projects.

Date and Time Columns

Date and Time:

- Description: Captures date and time values, with options to include just the date, or both date and time.

- Uses: Ideal for tracking deadlines, event dates, or timestamps. For example, in an event planning list, you might use this column to record event dates and times.

Choice Columns

Choice:

- Description: Allows you to create a predefined list of options that users can select from. You can choose between a dropdown menu, radio buttons, or checkboxes (for multiple selections).

- Uses: Useful for standardizing data entry with consistent options. In an employee directory list, this column could categorize employees by department.

Yes/No:

- Description: A simple binary choice column, typically displayed as a checkbox.

- Uses: Perfect for true/false or yes/no questions, such as tracking task completion or attendance. For instance, in a task management list, this column could indicate whether a task is completed.

Lookup Columns

Lookup:

- Description: Allows you to pull data from another list within the same site, creating a relationship between the two lists.

- Uses: Excellent for creating connections between lists, such as linking an employee list to a department list. In a project management scenario, you could link tasks to projects, pulling project names into the task list.

Person or Group Columns

Person or Group:

- Description: Enables you to select users or groups from your organization, often with options to display the name, email, or picture of the person.

- Uses: Useful for assigning tasks, tracking authorship, or identifying responsible parties. In a task list, this column could designate the person responsible for completing the task.

Hyperlink Columns

Hyperlink:

- Description: Stores URLs, with an option to include a display name.

- Uses: Ideal for linking to external resources, documents, or websites. In a resources list, this column could store links to important documents or reference materials.

Picture:

- Description: Similar to the Hyperlink column, but specifically for images. It allows you to display images directly within the list.

- Uses: Useful for visual references, such as product images or employee photos. In a product catalog list, this column could display images of the products.

Calculated Columns

Calculated:

- Description: Allows you to create a column based on a formula, using data from other columns in the list. These formulas can include mathematical operations, text concatenations, and logical comparisons.

- Uses: Perfect for automating calculations or generating dynamic content. For example, in an invoice list, a calculated column could automatically compute the total amount by multiplying the unit price by the quantity.

Managed Metadata Columns

Managed Metadata:

- Description: Leverages SharePoint's Term Store to provide a hierarchical set of terms that can be used across lists and libraries.

- Uses: Ideal for categorization and tagging, especially in scenarios requiring consistent taxonomy. In a document management system, this column could apply standardized tags to documents for easier retrieval.

Practical Applications and Examples

To further understand the utility of these column types, let's consider a few practical applications and examples across different use cases:

Project Management:

In a project management scenario, you might have a list to track various tasks. Here's how you could utilize different column types:

- Single Line of Text: Task Name

- Multiple Lines of Text: Task Description

- Number: Estimated Hours

- Currency: Budget

- Date and Time: Due Date

- Choice: Task Status (Not Started, In Progress, Completed)

- Person or Group: Assigned To

- Yes/No: Completed

- Calculated: Total Cost (Estimated Hours Hourly Rate)

Employee Directory:

For an employee directory, you could set up a list with the following columns:

- Single Line of Text: First Name

- Single Line of Text: Last Name

- Choice: Department (HR, IT, Sales, etc.)

- Number: Employee ID

- Date and Time: Hire Date

- Person or Group: Manager

- Hyperlink: LinkedIn Profile

- Picture: Employee Photo

Sales Tracking:

In a sales tracking scenario, a list might include:

- Single Line of Text: Product Name

- Choice: Product Category (Electronics, Furniture, Clothing, etc.)

- Number: Quantity Sold

- Currency: Unit Price

- Calculated: Total Revenue (Quantity Sold Unit Price)

- Date and Time: Sale Date

- Lookup: Sales Representative (from an employee list)

Event Planning:

For event planning, your list might look like this:

- Single Line of Text: Event Name

- Multiple Lines of Text: Event Description

- Date and Time: Event Date and Time

- Choice: Event Type (Conference, Webinar, Workshop, etc.)

- Person or Group: Event Organizer

- Yes/No: RSVP Required

- Hyperlink: Registration Link

- Picture: Event Banner

Customizing Columns for Better Data Management

Understanding the types of columns available is just the beginning. To make the most of Microsoft Lists, consider the following best practices for customizing columns:

1. Consistency: Use consistent naming conventions and data formats to ensure data integrity and ease of use.

2. Validation: Set up validation rules to prevent incorrect data entry. For example, ensure that dates are within a specific range or that numerical values meet certain criteria.

3. Default Values: Define default values for columns where appropriate to speed up data entry and ensure consistency.

4. Column Formatting: Utilize column formatting to visually differentiate important information. For instance, you can use conditional formatting to highlight overdue tasks or high-priority items.

5. Documentation: Document the purpose and usage of each column within your list to help users understand how to interact with the data effectively.

Conclusion

By leveraging the diverse range of column types in Microsoft Lists, you can create tailored lists that meet your specific data management needs. Whether you're tracking projects, managing employee information, or planning events, understanding and utilizing the appropriate column types will enhance your productivity and ensure your data is organized efficiently. As you become more familiar with these column types and their uses, you'll be able to customize your lists more effectively, leading to better data management and more streamlined workflows.

2.3 Using List Views

Creating Custom Views

Creating custom views in Microsoft Lists is an essential feature that allows users to tailor their list displays according to their specific needs and preferences. Custom views can significantly enhance data visibility and usability, enabling users to filter, sort, and present data in ways that make it easier to understand and act upon. This section will guide you through the process of creating custom views in Microsoft Lists, discussing various aspects including defining the view's purpose, selecting and arranging columns, applying filters and sorting, and using different view types.

Defining the Purpose of a Custom View

Before creating a custom view, it's important to define its purpose. Ask yourself what you want to achieve with this view. Are you looking to highlight specific information, streamline data entry, or facilitate reporting? Understanding the goal will help you make informed decisions about which data to include and how to present it.

For example, if you're managing a project and need to keep track of task statuses, a custom view that shows only incomplete tasks sorted by due date can help you stay on top of deadlines. Alternatively, if you're managing inventory, a view that highlights items with low stock levels can help you quickly identify what needs to be reordered.

Selecting and Arranging Columns

Once you have a clear purpose for your custom view, the next step is to select and arrange the columns that will be displayed. Microsoft Lists allows you to choose from existing columns or create new ones that are specific to your needs.

1. Selecting Columns: In the view settings, you can select the columns you want to display. It's important to choose columns that are relevant to the purpose of your view. For example, if you're creating a view for project tasks, you might include columns for Task Name, Assigned To, Due Date, and Status.

2. Arranging Columns: The order in which columns are displayed can impact how easily you can read and interpret the data. Arrange the columns in a logical sequence that aligns with your workflow. For instance, in a task management view, you might place the Task Name column first, followed by the Assigned To column, Due Date, and Status.

3. Column Widths: Adjusting column widths can also enhance the readability of your view. Ensure that important information is fully visible and that the layout is clean and uncluttered.

Applying Filters and Sorting

Custom views become particularly powerful when you apply filters and sorting. These tools allow you to narrow down your data to show only the most relevant information and to organize it in a meaningful way.

1. Filters: Filters enable you to display only the data that meets certain criteria. For example, you can filter tasks to show only those that are overdue or filter inventory items to show only those below a certain stock level. To apply a filter, go to the view settings and specify the conditions that must be met for an item to be included in the view.

2. Sorting: Sorting arranges the data in a specific order, making it easier to find what you're looking for. You can sort data alphabetically, numerically, or by date. For example, in a task management view, you might sort tasks by due date to see which tasks are coming up soonest. To sort data, go to the view settings and choose the column by which you want to sort, as well as the order (ascending or descending).

3. Combining Filters and Sorting: Combining filters and sorting can help you create highly customized views. For example, you can filter tasks to show only those assigned to a specific team member and then sort them by due date. This combination makes it easy for team members to focus on their own tasks and prioritize their work.

Using Different View Types

Microsoft Lists offers several view types, each with its own advantages. Depending on the nature of your data and the purpose of your custom view, you can choose the most appropriate view type.

1. Standard View: This is the default view type and is best for displaying data in a tabular format. It's ideal for lists that require a lot of detail, such as project tasks or inventory items.

The standard view allows for extensive customization, including column selection, filtering, and sorting.

2. Calendar View: The calendar view is perfect for displaying date-based information. It shows list items as events on a calendar, making it easy to visualize deadlines, appointments, and other time-sensitive data. This view is particularly useful for managing schedules, project timelines, and event planning.

3. Gallery View: The gallery view displays list items as cards, which can include images and key information. This view is great for visualizing items that have images or for presenting data in a more graphical format. It's commonly used for asset management, product catalogs, and portfolios.

4. Board View: The board view is designed for kanban-style task management. It organizes list items into columns based on status or another category, allowing you to move items between columns as their status changes. This view is highly effective for project management, agile workflows, and any process that involves moving tasks through different stages.

Creating a Custom View: Step-by-Step Guide

To create a custom view in Microsoft Lists, follow these steps:

1. Open the List: Start by opening the list for which you want to create a custom view.

2. Access View Options: Click on the "All items" dropdown at the top right of the list and select "Create new view."

3. Choose View Type: Select the type of view you want to create (Standard, Calendar, Gallery, or Board).

4. Name the View: Give your view a meaningful name that reflects its purpose.

5. Select Columns: Choose the columns you want to display in the view. You can add, remove, and rearrange columns as needed.

6. Apply Filters: Set up filters to narrow down the data displayed in the view. Specify the conditions that items must meet to be included.

7. Sort Data: Choose how you want to sort the data in the view. Select the column and order (ascending or descending).

8. Save the View: Once you've configured all the settings, click "Save" to create the custom view.

Practical Examples of Custom Views

To illustrate the power of custom views, let's look at a few practical examples:

1. Project Management View:

   - Purpose: To track tasks and deadlines for a project.

   - Columns: Task Name, Assigned To, Due Date, Status, Priority.

   - Filters: Show tasks with Status not equal to "Completed."

   - Sorting: Sort by Due Date in ascending order.

   - View Type: Standard.

2. Inventory Management View:

   - Purpose: To monitor stock levels and reorder items.

   - Columns: Item Name, Stock Level, Reorder Level, Supplier, Last Order Date.

   - Filters: Show items where Stock Level is less than Reorder Level.

   - Sorting: Sort by Stock Level in ascending order.

   - View Type: Standard.

3. Event Planning Calendar:

   - Purpose: To manage event schedules and deadlines.

   - Columns: Event Name, Date, Location, Organizer, Status.

   - Filters: Show events with Status not equal to "Cancelled."

   - Sorting: Not applicable for calendar view.

   - View Type: Calendar.

Tips for Effective Custom Views

To make the most of custom views in Microsoft Lists, consider the following tips:

1. Keep It Simple: Avoid cluttering your view with too many columns or complex filters. Focus on the most important data.

2. Use Descriptive Names: Give your views descriptive names that clearly indicate their purpose, making it easier to switch between views.

3. Test and Refine: After creating a custom view, test it to ensure it meets your needs. Refine the settings as necessary to improve usability.

4. Leverage Conditional Formatting: Use conditional formatting to highlight important data within your views, such as overdue tasks or low stock levels.

5. Regularly Review and Update: Periodically review your custom views to ensure they remain relevant and up-to-date with your changing needs.

By mastering the creation of custom views in Microsoft Lists, you can transform how you manage and interact with your data, making your workflow more efficient and your data more accessible.

Filtering and Sorting Data

One of the most powerful features of Microsoft Lists is the ability to filter and sort data to quickly find and analyze information. Properly utilizing filtering and sorting tools can significantly enhance your productivity, making it easier to manage and interpret your data.

Introduction to Filtering and Sorting

Filtering and sorting allow you to view your data in different ways, focusing on specific criteria and organizing the information to suit your needs. Filters let you display only the data that meets certain conditions, while sorting arranges your data in a specified order, either ascending or descending.

The Importance of Filtering and Sorting

Effective data management often depends on how well you can isolate and prioritize information. By filtering out unnecessary data and sorting it in a meaningful way, you can:

- Quickly locate specific records

- Analyze trends and patterns

- Improve decision-making processes

- Enhance reporting accuracy

- Streamline workflows

Getting Started with Filtering

Filtering in Microsoft Lists allows you to narrow down the data displayed based on specific criteria. This can be particularly useful when dealing with large datasets. Here's how you can apply filters in your lists:

1. Accessing the Filter Pane

  - Open your list and navigate to the view you want to filter.

  - Click on the "Filter" button in the command bar to open the filter pane on the right side of the screen.

2. Applying Basic Filters

  - In the filter pane, you'll see a list of columns that you can filter by.

  - Click on the column you want to filter.

  - Select the criteria you wish to apply. For example, if you are filtering by a "Status" column, you might select "Completed" to only show completed tasks.

  - The list will automatically update to show only the items that match your criteria.

3. Combining Multiple Filters

  - You can apply multiple filters simultaneously to narrow down your data further.

  - For instance, you might filter by "Status" and "Due Date" to see tasks that are completed and due within a certain timeframe.

- The filters work together to display only the items that meet all selected criteria.

4. Clearing Filters

- To remove a filter, simply click the "X" next to the filter criteria in the filter pane.

- You can also click "Clear All" to remove all applied filters and view the entire dataset again.

Advanced Filtering Techniques

Advanced filtering options allow for more complex queries and refined data views. These techniques can be particularly useful for in-depth data analysis.

1. Text Filters

- Use text filters to find items that contain, do not contain, start with, or end with specific text.

- For example, filter a "Title" column to find items that contain the word "Project."

2. Number Filters

- Apply numerical filters to columns with number data types.

- Options include filtering by greater than, less than, equal to, or between specific values.

- This is useful for budget tracking or performance metrics.

3. Date Filters

- Date filters help you find items within a specific time range.

- Options include filtering by before, after, or between certain dates.

- Use these filters for project deadlines or scheduling tasks.

4. Boolean Filters

- Boolean columns (Yes/No) can be filtered to show items that either match or do not match a given condition.

- This is useful for binary statuses like "Approved" or "Rejected."

5. Custom Filters

- Create custom filters by combining multiple conditions using AND/OR logic.

- For example, filter tasks that are either high priority or due within the next week.

Sorting Data

Sorting organizes your list items in a specific order, making it easier to analyze and manage your data. You can sort by any column, and the sort can be either ascending or descending.

1. Basic Sorting

  - Click on the column header you wish to sort by.

  - Choose "Sort Ascending" to arrange the data from smallest to largest or "Sort Descending" for the reverse.

  - For text columns, ascending sorts alphabetically A-Z, while descending sorts Z-A.

  - For numerical columns, ascending sorts from lowest to highest, and descending from highest to lowest.

  - For date columns, ascending sorts from oldest to newest, and descending from newest to oldest.

2. Multi-Level Sorting

  - Sometimes a single level of sorting isn't sufficient, especially with complex datasets.

  - Multi-level sorting allows you to sort by more than one column simultaneously.

  - To apply multi-level sorting:

    - Click the column header of the primary column you want to sort by.

    - Then, hold the "Shift" key and click the header of the second column you want to sort by.

    - This secondary sort will organize data within the already sorted primary column.

  - For example, you might first sort by "Priority" and then by "Due Date" within each priority level.

Combining Filtering and Sorting

For the most effective data management, combine filtering and sorting. This enables you to focus on specific subsets of data and organize them in a meaningful way.

1. Applying Filters and Sorts Together

  - First, apply your desired filters to narrow down the data.

  - Next, sort the filtered data to bring the most relevant items to the top.

  - This combination helps you quickly find and analyze the most important information.

2. Saving Filtered and Sorted Views

  - Once you have your data filtered and sorted to your liking, you can save this configuration as a new view.

  - Click on the view menu (usually labeled "All items" by default), and select "Save view as."

  - Name your new view and choose whether to make it public or private.

  - This saved view allows you to quickly return to your preferred data configuration without having to reapply filters and sorts each time.

 Practical Applications of Filtering and Sorting

Filtering and sorting are not just theoretical concepts; they have practical applications that can improve your daily workflow.

1. Task Management

  - Filter tasks by status (e.g., "In Progress," "Completed") to focus on what needs to be done.

  - Sort tasks by due date to prioritize urgent items.

2. Project Tracking

  - Filter projects by department or team to view relevant initiatives.

  - Sort projects by start date to see the timeline of upcoming work.

3. Sales Data Analysis

  - Filter sales records by region or product category to analyze specific markets.

- Sort sales by amount to identify top-performing products or sales representatives.

4. Customer Support

   - Filter support tickets by priority or status to manage workloads.

   - Sort tickets by creation date to address the oldest issues first.

5. Inventory Management

   - Filter inventory items by stock level to identify low-stock products.

   - Sort items by reorder date to streamline restocking processes.

Tips and Best Practices

To maximize the efficiency of filtering and sorting in Microsoft Lists, consider the following tips and best practices:

1. Use Descriptive Column Names

   - Ensure your column names clearly describe the data they contain. This makes filtering and sorting more intuitive.

2. Regularly Update Filters and Sorts

   - Your data needs may change over time, so regularly review and update your filters and sorts to ensure they remain relevant.

3. Leverage Conditional Formatting

   - Use conditional formatting to highlight important data, making it easier to spot trends and anomalies when filtering and sorting.

4. Save Frequently Used Views

   - Save views that you use regularly to avoid reapplying filters and sorts. This saves time and ensures consistency.

5. Train Team Members

   - Ensure all team members know how to use filtering and sorting features effectively. This enhances collaboration and data accuracy.

6. Monitor Performance

- Be mindful that extensive filtering and sorting on large datasets can impact performance. Optimize your lists to maintain efficiency.

Conclusion

Filtering and sorting are essential tools in Microsoft Lists that enable you to manage and analyze your data effectively. By mastering these techniques, you can improve your productivity, make informed decisions, and streamline your workflows. Whether you're managing tasks, tracking projects, analyzing sales, or handling customer support, filtering and sorting will help you organize your data in a way that best suits your needs. Remember to regularly update your filters and sorts, save useful views, and train your team to ensure everyone can benefit from these powerful features.

CHAPTER III
Advanced List Features

3.1 Integrating with Other Microsoft 365 Apps

Microsoft Lists is a powerful tool within the Microsoft 365 ecosystem, offering versatile functionalities for organizing and managing information. One of the significant advantages of using Microsoft Lists is its seamless integration with other Microsoft 365 applications. This integration enhances productivity and facilitates better collaboration across teams. In this section, we will explore how to integrate Microsoft Lists with Microsoft Teams, providing a detailed guide on connecting these two applications to maximize their potential.

Connecting Lists with Teams

Microsoft Teams is a collaboration hub that brings together chat, meetings, calls, and files into one unified platform. By integrating Microsoft Lists with Teams, you can streamline your workflow and improve team collaboration. Here's a step-by-step guide to connecting Microsoft Lists with Teams:

1. Understanding the Benefits of Integration

Before diving into the technical steps, it's essential to understand why integrating Lists with Teams is beneficial. Some of the key advantages include:

- Centralized Access: Teams allows users to access their lists directly within the chat interface, ensuring that all relevant information is easily accessible.

- Real-Time Collaboration: Teams' real-time chat and collaboration features complement the data management capabilities of Lists, making it easier for team members to discuss and update list items concurrently.

- Enhanced Productivity: By having Lists integrated into Teams, users can reduce context switching between different applications, thus saving time and enhancing productivity.

2. Adding a Microsoft List to a Team

To add a Microsoft List to a team in Microsoft Teams, follow these steps:

- Step 1: Open Microsoft Teams: Launch the Microsoft Teams application and navigate to the team where you want to add the list.

- Step 2: Select a Channel: Choose the channel within the team where the list will be added. Each channel can have multiple tabs for different applications and documents.

- Step 3: Add a Tab: Click on the "+" icon at the top of the channel to add a new tab.

- Step 4: Choose Microsoft Lists: In the Add a Tab dialog box, select "Microsoft Lists" from the list of available applications.

- Step 5: Create or Add an Existing List:

  - Create a New List: If you want to create a new list, select "Create a list." You will be prompted to choose a template or start from blank.

  - Add an Existing List: To add an existing list, select "Add an existing list." You can then choose a list from your recent lists or from any SharePoint site you have access to.

3. Customizing the List Tab

Once the list is added to the channel, you can customize the tab to fit your needs:

- Rename the Tab: By default, the tab will be named "Lists." You can rename it to something more descriptive by right-clicking the tab and selecting "Rename."

- Configure List Settings: Click on the tab to open the list and configure settings such as views, filters, and formatting to suit your team's requirements.

- Permissions and Access Control: Ensure that the appropriate permissions are set so that all team members can access and edit the list as needed.

4. Collaborating on Lists within Teams

With the list integrated into Teams, collaboration becomes more seamless:

- Discuss List Items in Chat: Team members can discuss specific list items directly within the Teams chat. Use the @mention feature to tag colleagues and bring their attention to particular list entries.

- Edit List Items in Real-Time: Multiple users can edit list items simultaneously, with changes being updated in real-time. This ensures that everyone is always working with the latest data.

- Use Teams Features for List Management: Leverage Teams features such as channel notifications, file sharing, and meeting scheduling to enhance your list management processes.

5. Best Practices for Using Lists in Teams

To get the most out of your Lists integration with Teams, consider the following best practices:

- Regularly Update and Review Lists: Ensure that your lists are kept up-to-date and are regularly reviewed for accuracy. Use Teams notifications to remind team members of updates.

- Create Custom Views for Different Needs: Utilize custom views to display list data in ways that are most relevant to different stakeholders. For instance, create a view for project managers that highlights deadlines and priorities.

- Leverage Power Automate for Workflows: Integrate Power Automate to create workflows that automate repetitive tasks, such as sending notifications when a list item is updated or moving items to different lists based on specific criteria.

6. Troubleshooting and Support

While integrating Microsoft Lists with Teams is generally straightforward, you may encounter some issues. Here are some common problems and solutions:

- List Not Displaying Properly: Ensure that you have the necessary permissions to access the list. Check the list settings in SharePoint to confirm that it is shared with the correct team members.

- Synchronization Issues: If changes made in Teams are not reflecting in the list, try refreshing the Teams application. Ensure that you have a stable internet connection.

- Permissions Problems: Verify that the list permissions in SharePoint match the intended access levels for team members in Teams.

7. Real-World Use Cases

To illustrate the practical applications of integrating Microsoft Lists with Teams, consider these real-world scenarios:

- Project Management: A project team uses a list to track tasks, deadlines, and responsibilities. By integrating the list into their project's Teams channel, they can easily update task statuses, discuss issues, and ensure everyone is on the same page.

- Customer Support: A customer support team maintains a list of support tickets and their statuses. Integrating this list with Teams allows support agents to quickly update ticket statuses, collaborate on difficult cases, and provide timely updates to customers.

- Event Planning: An event planning team uses a list to manage event details, vendor contacts, and schedules. By integrating the list with Teams, they can streamline communication with vendors, track event milestones, and coordinate logistics effectively.

Conclusion

Integrating Microsoft Lists with Microsoft Teams unlocks a powerful synergy that enhances team collaboration and productivity. By following the steps outlined in this section, you can seamlessly connect your lists with Teams and take full advantage of the combined capabilities of these two applications. Whether you are managing projects, handling customer support, or planning events, the integration of Lists with Teams will help you stay organized, informed, and efficient.

Using Lists with Power Automate

Integrating Microsoft Lists with Power Automate can significantly enhance your productivity and streamline various workflows. Power Automate, formerly known as Microsoft Flow, is a cloud-based service that allows users to create automated workflows between different applications and services. This integration enables you to automate repetitive tasks, set up complex business processes, and ensure that data flows smoothly across different Microsoft 365 applications and other services. In this section, we will explore how to leverage Power Automate to maximize the potential of Microsoft Lists.

Understanding Power Automate

Power Automate is designed to help users create workflows that can automate tasks and processes. These workflows, called "flows," can range from simple automations to complex, multi-step processes that involve various applications. Power Automate offers a user-friendly interface, with a variety of templates and connectors that make it easy to get started with creating flows.

Key Features of Power Automate

1. Templates and Connectors: Power Automate provides a vast library of templates and connectors for various applications and services. These templates can be used as starting points for creating your own flows.

2. Triggers and Actions: Flows are built using triggers and actions. Triggers initiate the flow based on specific events, while actions define what the flow will do once triggered.

3. Conditional Logic: You can incorporate conditional logic into your flows, allowing for more complex decision-making processes within your workflows.

4. Approvals: Power Automate includes built-in approval workflows, which can be used to automate approval processes for various tasks and requests.

5. Integration with Microsoft 365: Power Automate seamlessly integrates with Microsoft 365 applications, making it easy to create workflows that involve SharePoint, Outlook, Teams, and, of course, Microsoft Lists.

Setting Up Power Automate with Microsoft Lists

To begin integrating Microsoft Lists with Power Automate, you'll need access to both services through your Microsoft 365 subscription. Here's a step-by-step guide to get started:

1. Accessing Power Automate: You can access Power Automate from the Microsoft 365 app launcher or directly at powerautomate.microsoft.com.

2. Creating a New Flow: In Power Automate, select "Create" to start a new flow. You'll be prompted to choose from different types of flows: automated flow, instant flow, scheduled flow, and business process flow. For integrating with Microsoft Lists, an automated flow or instant flow is typically used.

3. Choosing a Trigger: Select a trigger that will initiate your flow. For Microsoft Lists, common triggers include "When an item is created" or "When an item is modified." These triggers can be found under the SharePoint or Microsoft Lists connectors.

4. Adding Actions: After setting up the trigger, you can start adding actions to your flow. Actions define what happens after the trigger event. For instance, you can send an email, create a task in Planner, or update an item in another list.

Example Workflow: Automating Task Creation

Let's create a flow that automatically creates a task in Microsoft Planner when a new item is added to a Microsoft List.

1. Choose the Trigger: Select the "When an item is created" trigger from the SharePoint or Microsoft Lists connector.

2. Specify the List: Configure the trigger by specifying the site address and the list name where the new item will be created.

3. Add an Action: Click on "New Step" and choose the "Create a task" action from the Planner connector.

4. Configure the Task: Fill in the required details for the Planner task, such as the Plan Id, Task Title, and any other relevant fields. You can use dynamic content from the Microsoft List item to populate these fields.

5. Save and Test: Save your flow and test it by adding a new item to your specified Microsoft List. The flow should trigger automatically and create a new task in Planner based on the item details.

Advanced Automation Scenarios

Once you're comfortable with basic automations, you can explore more advanced scenarios that leverage the full potential of Power Automate.

Conditional Logic and Approvals

You can add conditional logic to your flows to handle different scenarios based on the data in your Microsoft Lists. For example, you might want to set up an approval workflow where a manager needs to approve certain items before they are added to a list.

1. Adding Conditions: After your initial action, click "New Step" and choose "Condition" to add a conditional statement. You can configure the condition to check specific fields in your Microsoft List item.

2. Setting Up Approval Steps: If the condition is met, you can add an "Approval" action. Configure the approval process by specifying the approvers and the details of the approval request.

3. Handling Approval Outcomes: Based on the approval outcome, you can define further actions. For example, if the item is approved, it might be moved to another list or updated with additional information.

Integrating with External Services

Power Automate's connectors allow you to integrate Microsoft Lists with a wide range of external services. This can be particularly useful for automating workflows that span multiple platforms.

1. Connecting to Third-Party Services: You can use connectors for services like Slack, Trello, or Salesforce to create cross-platform automations. For instance, you can create a Trello card or send a Slack message when an item in a Microsoft List is updated.

2. Using HTTP Requests: For more advanced integrations, you can use HTTP requests to interact with APIs. This allows for highly customized workflows that can interact with virtually any web service.

Error Handling and Monitoring

To ensure that your flows run smoothly, it's important to implement error handling and monitoring mechanisms.

1. Adding Error Handling Steps: Power Automate allows you to add steps that handle errors in your flow. You can configure these steps to run only if previous actions fail, allowing you to log errors or notify administrators.

2. Monitoring Flows: Power Automate provides tools to monitor the performance and status of your flows. You can view the run history, check for failures, and see detailed logs for troubleshooting.

Best Practices for Using Power Automate with Microsoft Lists

To get the most out of integrating Microsoft Lists with Power Automate, consider the following best practices:

1. Start with Templates: Use Power Automate templates as starting points for your flows. This can save time and provide inspiration for creating your own custom workflows.

2. Test Thoroughly: Always test your flows thoroughly in a development environment before deploying them to production. This helps ensure that they work as expected and reduces the risk of disruptions.

3. Document Your Flows: Maintain clear documentation for each flow you create. This should include the purpose of the flow, the triggers and actions used, and any special configurations. Documentation helps with maintenance and troubleshooting.

4. Regularly Review and Update: Periodically review and update your flows to ensure they remain effective and aligned with your business processes. As your organization evolves, your workflows may need adjustments.

5. Monitor and Optimize Performance: Keep an eye on the performance of your flows. Look for opportunities to optimize steps, reduce execution time, and improve reliability.

Conclusion

Integrating Microsoft Lists with Power Automate opens up a world of possibilities for automating and streamlining your workflows. By leveraging the powerful features of Power Automate, you can create sophisticated automations that enhance productivity, reduce manual effort, and ensure seamless data integration across your organization. Whether you are just starting with simple flows or exploring advanced automation scenarios, Power Automate provides the tools you need to get organized and stay efficient with Microsoft Lists.

3.2 Setting Up Alerts and Notifications

Creating Alerts for List Items

One of the powerful features of Microsoft Lists is the ability to create alerts for list items. Alerts are essential for staying informed about changes and updates to your lists, ensuring that you and your team are always up-to-date. In this section, we will explore how to create and manage alerts for list items, offering step-by-step instructions and best practices to maximize their effectiveness.

Why Create Alerts for List Items?

Creating alerts for list items in Microsoft Lists can significantly enhance your productivity and collaboration. Here are a few reasons why setting up alerts is beneficial:

1. Timely Updates: Alerts notify you immediately when changes occur, ensuring you are always aware of important updates.

2. Improved Collaboration: Alerts help team members stay informed about changes, promoting better coordination and collaboration.

3. Increased Efficiency: By receiving alerts, you can quickly respond to changes and updates, reducing delays and improving workflow efficiency.

4. Error Reduction: Alerts can help prevent errors by notifying you of potential issues or discrepancies in real-time.

Creating Alerts for List Items: Step-by-Step Guide

Creating alerts in Microsoft Lists is a straightforward process. Follow these steps to set up alerts for your list items:

1. Navigate to Your List: Open the Microsoft Lists app and select the list for which you want to create alerts.

2. Access List Settings: Click on the three-dot menu (ellipsis) in the upper-right corner of the list and select "Alert me" from the dropdown menu.

3. Configure Alert Settings:

  - Alert Title: Provide a descriptive title for your alert. This title will help you identify the alert in the future.

  - Send Alerts To: Specify the email addresses of the individuals who should receive the alerts. You can add multiple email addresses separated by semicolons.

  - Delivery Method: Choose the delivery method for your alerts. You can select email, SMS, or both, depending on your preferences and the available options.

4. Set Alert Conditions:

  - Alert Type: Choose the type of changes that will trigger the alert. Options include "All changes," "New items are added," "Existing items are modified," or "Items are deleted."

  - Send Alerts For These Changes: Define the specific conditions that will trigger the alert. For example, you can choose to receive alerts only when changes are made to specific columns or fields.

5. Specify Alert Frequency:

  - Send Notification Immediately: Select this option if you want to receive alerts as soon as changes occur.

  - Send a Daily Summary: Choose this option to receive a daily summary of all changes made to the list.

  - Send a Weekly Summary: Opt for a weekly summary if you prefer to receive updates on a weekly basis.

6. Save Alert Settings: Once you have configured all the alert settings, click "OK" or "Save" to create the alert. You will receive a confirmation message indicating that the alert has been successfully created.

Best Practices for Creating Alerts

To ensure that your alerts are effective and useful, consider the following best practices:

1. Use Descriptive Titles: When creating an alert, use a descriptive title that clearly indicates the purpose of the alert. This will help you and your team easily identify the alert in the future.

2. Target Specific Changes: Instead of creating alerts for all changes, focus on specific changes that are most relevant to your workflow. This will help you avoid unnecessary notifications and stay focused on important updates.

3. Limit the Number of Recipients: Only include individuals who need to be informed about the changes in the recipient list. This will reduce the chances of alert fatigue and ensure that the right people receive the notifications.

4. Adjust Alert Frequency: Depending on the nature of your list and the frequency of changes, choose an appropriate alert frequency. For lists with frequent updates, immediate notifications might be useful, while for less active lists, daily or weekly summaries might be more appropriate.

5. Regularly Review and Update Alerts: Periodically review your alert settings to ensure they are still relevant and useful. Update or delete alerts that are no longer needed to keep your notifications streamlined and effective.

Example Scenarios for Creating Alerts

To illustrate the practical application of creating alerts in Microsoft Lists, let's consider a few example scenarios:

1. Project Management: You are managing a project with multiple tasks and team members. By creating alerts for task updates, you can ensure that you are immediately notified when a task is completed, assigned, or updated, allowing you to manage the project more efficiently.

2. Inventory Tracking: You maintain an inventory list to track stock levels. By setting up alerts for low stock levels, you can receive notifications when the quantity of an item falls below a certain threshold, enabling you to reorder supplies in a timely manner.

3. Customer Support: Your team uses a list to track customer support tickets. By creating alerts for new tickets, you can ensure that support agents are promptly notified of incoming requests, improving response times and customer satisfaction.

4. Compliance Monitoring: You have a compliance checklist list that requires regular updates. By setting up alerts for checklist items, you can receive notifications when items are added, updated, or marked as complete, helping you stay on top of compliance requirements.

Managing and Modifying Alerts

Once you have created alerts, you might need to modify or manage them based on changing requirements. Here's how you can manage and modify your alerts in Microsoft Lists:

1. Access Alert Settings: Navigate to the list for which you have created alerts and click on the three-dot menu (ellipsis). Select "Manage my alerts" from the dropdown menu.

2. View Existing Alerts: You will see a list of all the alerts you have created for the selected list. Click on the alert you want to modify.

3. Edit Alert Settings: In the alert settings window, make the necessary changes to the alert configuration, such as updating the alert title, recipients, conditions, or frequency.

4. Save Changes: After making the desired modifications, click "OK" or "Save" to apply the changes. Your alert will be updated accordingly.

5. Delete Alerts: If you no longer need a particular alert, select the alert from the list and click "Delete" to remove it.

Conclusion

Creating alerts for list items in Microsoft Lists is a powerful feature that can help you stay informed and responsive to changes. By following the steps outlined in this section, you can set up and manage alerts effectively, ensuring that you and your team are always aware of important updates. With best practices and practical examples, you can leverage alerts to enhance productivity, improve collaboration, and streamline your workflows.

Managing Notifications

Introduction

Managing notifications is a crucial aspect of maintaining efficiency and ensuring that team members stay informed about relevant updates and changes within Microsoft Lists. Notifications help users to stay on top of important list activities, ensuring that they are promptly aware of any changes, tasks, or items that require their attention. This section will delve into the intricacies of managing notifications effectively in Microsoft Lists, covering the types of notifications available, how to customize them, and best practices for ensuring that notifications are both useful and non-intrusive.

Types of Notifications

Microsoft Lists offers several types of notifications designed to keep users informed about list activities:

1. Email Notifications: These notifications are sent directly to the user's email address, providing detailed information about changes or updates.

2. In-App Notifications: These notifications appear within the Microsoft Lists interface, alerting users to changes when they are working within the app.

3. Mobile Notifications: For users who have the Microsoft Lists mobile app, notifications can be sent directly to their mobile device, ensuring they stay informed on the go.

Setting Up Notifications

To manage notifications effectively, it is essential to first understand how to set them up. Notifications can be configured for different types of list activities, such as item changes, comments, and workflow updates.

1. Accessing Notification Settings:

  - Open the list for which you want to manage notifications.

  - Click on the settings icon (gear icon) in the top right corner.

  - Select "List settings" from the dropdown menu.

  - In the list settings page, find the "Notification settings" section.

2. Configuring Email Notifications:

  - Within the notification settings, select "Email notifications."

  - Choose the events you want to receive email notifications for, such as item creation, item modification, and item deletion.

  - Specify the email addresses of the recipients. You can add multiple email addresses if multiple team members need to be notified.

- Customize the email message template to include relevant information and context.

3. Setting Up In-App Notifications:

   - In the notification settings, select "In-App notifications."

   - Similar to email notifications, choose the events you want to be notified about within the app.

   - Customize the notification preferences to control how they appear, such as pop-up alerts or subtle indicators.

4. Enabling Mobile Notifications:

   - Ensure that the Microsoft Lists mobile app is installed on your device.

   - In the app, navigate to the list for which you want to enable notifications.

   - Go to the settings menu and select "Mobile notifications."

   - Choose the types of notifications you want to receive on your mobile device and customize the settings as needed.

Customizing Notification Preferences

Effective notification management involves customizing preferences to ensure that notifications are relevant and helpful without being overwhelming. Here are some ways to customize notification preferences:

1. Frequency of Notifications:

   - Determine how often you want to receive notifications. Options might include real-time, daily summaries, or weekly digests.

   - For critical updates, real-time notifications may be necessary, while less urgent updates might be better suited to daily or weekly summaries.

2. Filtering Notifications:

   - Use filters to receive notifications only for specific types of list items or activities. For example, you might want notifications only for high-priority tasks or changes made by specific team members.

- Implement conditional logic to refine notifications further, ensuring that only relevant updates are communicated.

3. Notification Channels:

- Decide whether you want to receive notifications via email, in-app alerts, or mobile push notifications. You can choose one or a combination of these channels based on your preferences and working style.

- Customize the notification content for each channel to ensure that it is optimized for the medium (e.g., concise messages for mobile notifications).

4. Managing Notification Settings for Different Lists:

- Different lists may require different notification settings based on their purpose and audience. Customize the settings for each list individually to ensure that notifications are tailored to the specific needs of each list.

- Review and adjust notification settings periodically to accommodate changes in team structure, project priorities, or workflow processes.

Best Practices for Notification Management

To maximize the effectiveness of notifications while minimizing potential distractions, consider the following best practices:

1. Prioritizing Important Notifications:

- Focus on notifications that are critical to your workflow or project. Prioritize notifications for high-priority tasks, deadlines, and key updates.

- Use color-coding or other visual indicators to distinguish important notifications from less urgent ones.

2. Avoiding Notification Overload:

- Limit the number of notifications you receive to avoid becoming overwhelmed. Too many notifications can lead to important updates being overlooked.

- Set up filters and rules to ensure that you only receive notifications for the most relevant and actionable updates.

3. Ensuring Clarity and Context:

- Customize notification messages to provide clear and concise information. Include context such as the nature of the update, the list item affected, and any actions required.

- Use templates to standardize notification messages and ensure consistency across different types of notifications.

4. Regularly Reviewing and Adjusting Settings:

- Periodically review your notification settings to ensure they are still aligned with your needs and preferences. Adjust settings as necessary to accommodate changes in your workflow or team structure.

- Solicit feedback from team members to identify any issues with notifications and make adjustments to improve the overall notification system.

5. Training and Communication:

- Provide training and guidance to team members on how to manage their own notification settings. Encourage them to customize their notifications to suit their individual preferences and roles.

- Maintain open communication about notification preferences and encourage team members to share any challenges or suggestions for improvement.

Use Cases and Scenarios

To illustrate the practical application of notification management, consider the following use cases and scenarios:

1. Project Management:

- In a project management scenario, set up notifications for task assignments, deadline changes, and milestone completions. Ensure that project managers and team members are promptly informed about critical updates.

- Use daily summaries to provide an overview of project progress and any outstanding tasks.

2. Collaborative Editing:

- For lists used for collaborative editing, such as content calendars or document reviews, enable notifications for comments and edits made by team members. This ensures that everyone stays informed about changes and can respond promptly.

- Set up in-app notifications to provide real-time updates while working within the list.

3. Inventory Management:

- In an inventory management scenario, use notifications to alert team members about low stock levels, new stock arrivals, and inventory adjustments. This helps maintain accurate inventory records and prevents stockouts.

- Customize notifications to include relevant details such as item names, quantities, and actions required.

4. Customer Support:

- For lists used in customer support, set up notifications for new support tickets, status updates, and resolution comments. Ensure that support agents and managers are informed about new and ongoing issues.

- Use mobile notifications to keep support agents informed while they are on the move.

Conclusion

Managing notifications in Microsoft Lists is a powerful way to stay informed and maintain efficiency in various workflows. By understanding the types of notifications available, customizing preferences, and following best practices, users can ensure that they receive relevant updates without becoming overwhelmed. Whether for project management, collaborative editing, inventory management, or customer support, effective notification management is key to leveraging the full potential of Microsoft Lists. Regularly reviewing and adjusting notification settings, prioritizing important updates, and providing training to team members are essential steps in creating a streamlined and productive notification system.

3.3 Using Rules and Automations

Automating processes within Microsoft Lists is a powerful way to ensure efficiency and consistency across your organization. Automations can save time by handling repetitive tasks and ensuring that critical steps are never missed. In this section, we will explore how to create simple rules that can automatically trigger actions based on specific conditions.

Creating Simple Rules

Creating simple rules in Microsoft Lists is an accessible and effective way to streamline your workflows. These rules are designed to automate actions based on certain conditions, such as sending notifications, updating list items, or creating new tasks. Let's delve into the process of setting up these rules, step by step.

Introduction to Rules

Rules in Microsoft Lists are essentially predefined conditions that, when met, trigger specific actions. This automation can help reduce manual effort, minimize errors, and ensure timely responses to important changes within your lists. Before we get into creating rules, it's important to understand the basic components of a rule:

1. Condition: This defines the criteria that must be met for the rule to be triggered. Conditions can be based on various factors such as the status of a list item, specific dates, or changes made to list fields.

2. Action: This specifies what happens when the condition is met. Actions can include sending an email, updating a list item, or creating a task in another application.

Setting Up Simple Rules

To create a simple rule in Microsoft Lists, follow these steps:

1. Accessing the Rule Creation Interface: Navigate to the list where you want to create the rule. Click on the "Automate" button in the command bar, and then select "Create a rule."

2. Selecting a Trigger Condition: The first step in creating a rule is to define the trigger condition. Microsoft Lists offers several predefined conditions such as:

- When an item is created

- When an item is modified

- When a column value changes

Select the appropriate condition based on your requirement. For example, if you want a rule that triggers when a new item is created, select "When an item is created."

3. Defining the Condition Details: Depending on the trigger condition selected, you may need to provide additional details. For instance, if you chose "When a column value changes," you need to specify which column and the type of change (e.g., "Status" changes to "Completed").

4. Choosing an Action: After defining the condition, the next step is to specify the action. Microsoft Lists provides various actions such as:

- Send an email notification

- Update item

- Create a task

Select the action that best suits your needs. For instance, to send an email notification when a new item is created, choose "Send an email."

5. Configuring Action Details: Once the action is selected, configure the details. For sending an email notification, you need to specify the recipients, subject, and body of the email. You can use dynamic content from the list item to personalize the email. For example, include the item title or creator's name in the email body.

6. Saving and Activating the Rule: Review the condition and action configuration to ensure everything is set up correctly. Click "Save" to create the rule. The rule will be active immediately, and the specified actions will trigger whenever the condition is met.

Practical Examples of Simple Rules

Let's explore a few practical examples of simple rules to illustrate how they can be applied effectively:

1. Example 1: Notification for New Items

   - Condition: When an item is created

   - Action: Send an email notification

   - Details: Send an email to the project manager whenever a new task is added to the project list. Include the task title, description, and due date in the email body.

   Implementation:

   - Navigate to the project list.

   - Click on "Automate" > "Create a rule."

   - Select "When an item is created."

   - Choose "Send an email" as the action.

   - Configure the email details with dynamic content.

   - Save the rule.

2. Example 2: Status Update Alert

   - Condition: When a column value changes

   - Action: Send a notification

   - Details: Notify the assigned team member when the task status changes to "Completed."

   Implementation:

   - Open the task list.

   - Click on "Automate" > "Create a rule."

   - Select "When a column value changes."

   - Specify the column "Status" and the condition "changes to Completed."

   - Choose "Send a notification" as the action.

   - Configure the notification details with dynamic content.

   - Save the rule.

3. Example 3: Due Date Reminder

- Condition: When an item is due in 3 days

- Action: Send an email reminder

- Details: Send a reminder email to the task owner 3 days before the task due date.

Implementation:

- Go to the task list.

- Click on "Automate" > "Create a rule."

- Select "When an item is due in 3 days."

- Choose "Send an email reminder" as the action.

- Configure the email details with dynamic content.

- Save the rule.

Managing and Editing Rules

Once you have created rules, you may need to manage or edit them to ensure they continue to meet your needs. Here's how to do it:

1. Viewing Existing Rules: To see a list of all rules created for a list, click on "Automate" > "Manage rules." This will display all active rules along with their conditions and actions.

2. Editing a Rule: If you need to change a rule, select it from the list of existing rules and click "Edit." Make the necessary changes to the condition or action, and then save the updated rule.

3. Deleting a Rule: If a rule is no longer needed, you can delete it by selecting the rule and clicking "Delete." Confirm the deletion to remove the rule permanently.

4. Disabling a Rule: If you want to temporarily stop a rule without deleting it, you can disable it. Select the rule and click "Disable." You can re-enable it later if needed.

Best Practices for Creating Simple Rules

To maximize the effectiveness of rules in Microsoft Lists, consider the following best practices:

1. Start Simple: Begin with basic rules to automate common tasks. As you become more comfortable, you can create more complex rules with multiple conditions and actions.

2. Test Rules Thoroughly: Before relying on a rule, test it thoroughly to ensure it behaves as expected. Check that the conditions trigger correctly and the actions perform as intended.

3. Document Your Rules: Maintain a record of all rules created for each list. Document the conditions, actions, and purpose of each rule. This will help you manage and troubleshoot rules more effectively.

4. Review and Update Regularly: Periodically review your rules to ensure they are still relevant and effective. Update or remove outdated rules to keep your automation streamlined.

5. Use Dynamic Content Wisely: When configuring actions like email notifications, use dynamic content to personalize the messages. This ensures the recipients receive relevant and context-specific information.

Conclusion

Creating simple rules in Microsoft Lists is a powerful way to enhance productivity and efficiency. By automating routine tasks, you can focus on more strategic activities and ensure consistency in your processes. With the steps and best practices outlined in this section, you are well-equipped to start leveraging rules to streamline your workflows.

In the next section, we will explore advanced automations using Power Automate, enabling you to create more sophisticated and multi-step workflows that integrate seamlessly with other Microsoft 365 apps and services. Stay tuned to unlock the full potential of automation with Microsoft Lists!

Advanced Automations with Power Automate

Power Automate, formerly known as Microsoft Flow, is a powerful tool within the Microsoft 365 suite that allows users to automate workflows between various applications and services. When integrated with Microsoft Lists, Power Automate can significantly enhance the functionality and efficiency of your lists by automating repetitive tasks, connecting with other systems, and ensuring that your data processes are streamlined and consistent. This section will guide you through creating advanced automations using Power Automate, providing practical examples and best practices to help you get the most out of this powerful tool.

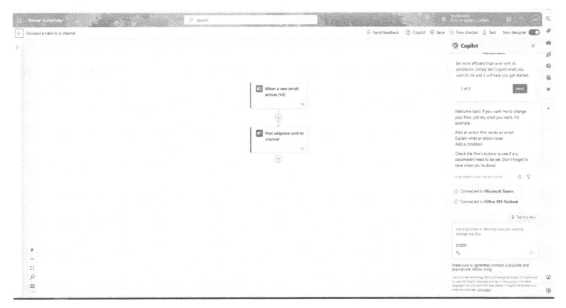

Overview of Power Automate

Power Automate allows users to create automated workflows, known as flows, which can perform a wide range of actions based on specified triggers. These flows can interact with over 300 different applications and services, including Microsoft Lists, SharePoint, Outlook, Teams, and many more. The types of flows that can be created include:

- Automated Flows: Triggered by specific events, such as an item being added to a list.

- Button Flows: Manually triggered by a user.

- Scheduled Flows: Triggered at a specified time or interval.

- Business Process Flows: Guided, multi-step processes.

Setting Up Power Automate

To get started with Power Automate, navigate to the Power Automate portal at flow.microsoft.com. Sign in with your Microsoft 365 account. If you haven't used Power Automate before, take a moment to explore the interface and familiarize yourself with the key components, such as the navigation pane, flow templates, and the flow creation tools.

Creating Advanced Flows for Microsoft Lists

To illustrate the capabilities of Power Automate, we'll create an advanced flow that performs multiple actions based on changes to a Microsoft List. The example will cover the following scenario:

- When a new item is added to a list, check specific conditions.

- If the conditions are met, update the item and send notifications to relevant users.

- Log the changes in another list for audit purposes.

Step 1: Create a New Automated Flow

1. In the Power Automate portal, select Create from the left-hand navigation pane.

2. Choose Automated flow.

3. Give your flow a name, such as "Advanced List Automation", and select the trigger When an item is created from Microsoft Lists.

4. Click Create to open the flow designer.

Step 2: Configure the Trigger

1. In the flow designer, specify the site address and list name where the trigger should apply.

2. Add the necessary fields that will be monitored for changes. For example, you might select fields like "Title", "Status", and "Priority".

Step 3: Add Conditions to the Flow

1. Click on New step and choose Condition.

2. Define the condition that needs to be met. For instance, if the "Status" field is equal to "Pending" and the "Priority" field is "High".

3. Set up the condition's logic to evaluate these criteria.

Step 4: Define Actions for the Condition

If Yes:

1. Update the Item:

   - Choose Update item action from Microsoft Lists.

   - Specify the list and the item ID, and then set the fields you want to update, such as changing the "Status" to "In Progress".

2. Send Notifications:

   - Choose Send an email (V2) action from Office 365 Outlook.

   - Specify the recipients, subject, and body of the email. Include dynamic content from the list item to personalize the message.

3. Log Changes:

   - Choose Create item action from Microsoft Lists.

   - Specify another list (Audit Log) where changes should be logged.

   - Set fields like "Change Type", "Original Value", "New Value", and "Changed By".

If No:

1. Send a Notification:

   - Choose Send an email (V2) action from Office 365 Outlook.

   - Notify the relevant user that the item did not meet the criteria for processing.

Step 5: Test the Flow

1. Save the flow and go back to your Microsoft List.

2. Add a new item to the list that matches the condition criteria.

3. Observe the automated actions taking place: the item should be updated, emails should be sent, and the change should be logged in the audit list.

Best Practices for Advanced Automations

1. Start Simple: Begin with basic flows and gradually add complexity as you become more comfortable with Power Automate.

2. Use Templates: Explore Power Automate templates to find pre-built flows that you can customize to suit your needs.

3. Document Your Flows: Keep a record of your flows, their purposes, and their configurations. This will help in troubleshooting and maintaining them over time.

4. Test Thoroughly: Always test your flows with various scenarios to ensure they work as expected and handle all possible edge cases.

5. Monitor and Maintain: Regularly review the performance of your flows. Check for any errors or issues and make necessary adjustments.

Advanced Use Cases for Power Automate with Microsoft Lists

1. Approval Workflows:

  - Automate multi-step approval processes where list items must be reviewed and approved by multiple stakeholders.

  - Use the Start and wait for an approval action to create approval requests, track responses, and take actions based on approvals or rejections.

2. Data Integration:

  - Integrate Microsoft Lists with other data sources such as SQL databases, CRM systems, or other external applications.

  - Use the Get rows action to retrieve data from external sources and populate your lists.

3. Reporting and Analytics:

  - Create automated reports by exporting list data to Excel or Power BI.

  - Use the Run query and list rows present in a table actions to extract data and generate reports on a scheduled basis.

4. Automated Reminders:

- Set up reminder emails for tasks or events with approaching deadlines.

- Use the Schedule - Recurrence trigger to periodically check the list for upcoming due dates and send reminders accordingly.

Conclusion

Advanced automations with Power Automate can transform the way you use Microsoft Lists by reducing manual effort, ensuring data consistency, and improving overall efficiency. By leveraging the power of automated workflows, you can focus on more strategic tasks and leave the repetitive, time-consuming activities to Power Automate.

As you continue to explore and implement automations, remember to stay updated with new features and enhancements in Power Automate and Microsoft Lists. The integration between these tools is continually evolving, offering even more opportunities to streamline and optimize your workflows.

CHAPTER IV
Collaborating with Microsoft Lists

4.1 Sharing Lists with Others

Permissions and Access Control

Microsoft Lists is a powerful tool for organizing and managing information, but its true potential is unlocked when used collaboratively. Sharing lists with team members or other stakeholders is essential for effective teamwork, enabling everyone to access, contribute, and utilize the data efficiently. To ensure that the right people have the appropriate access while maintaining data security and integrity, understanding and managing permissions and access control is crucial.

Understanding Permissions and Access Control

Permissions and access control in Microsoft Lists revolve around who can view, edit, and manage lists and list items. Microsoft Lists leverages the robust permissions infrastructure of SharePoint, allowing for fine-grained control over user access. The key components include:

1. Site Permissions: Microsoft Lists is built on SharePoint, meaning list permissions are managed at the site level. Each SharePoint site has its own set of permissions that cascade down to the lists within it.

2. List Permissions: Within a site, specific lists can have unique permissions. This is useful for scenarios where certain lists require restricted access, even if other lists within the same site are more widely accessible.

3. Item-Level Permissions: For even more granular control, permissions can be set at the individual item level within a list. This ensures that sensitive data within a list is only accessible to authorized users.

Configuring Permissions for Microsoft Lists

1. Accessing List Permissions Settings

   To configure permissions for a list, follow these steps:

   - Navigate to the SharePoint site where your list is located.

   - Go to the list you want to manage.

   - Click on the settings gear icon in the upper-right corner and select "List settings."

   - Under "Permissions and Management," click on "Permissions for this list."

2. Understanding Permission Levels

   SharePoint provides several default permission levels that can be assigned to users or groups. The most common levels include:

   - Full Control: Users can manage the site, including creating, editing, and deleting lists and list items.

   - Edit: Users can add, edit, and delete list items and documents.

   - Contribute: Users can add and edit list items and documents, but not delete them.

   - Read: Users can view list items and documents but cannot make any changes.

   - Limited Access: Users have access to a specific item or document but cannot view or edit anything else in the list or site.

3. Granting Permissions

   To grant permissions to users or groups:

   - In the list permissions settings, click on the "Grant Permissions" button.

   - Enter the names or email addresses of the users or groups you want to grant permissions to.

   - Select the appropriate permission level from the dropdown menu.

- Optionally, you can include a personal message to notify users of their new permissions.

- Click "Share" to apply the permissions.

4. Creating Custom Permission Levels

While the default permission levels cover most scenarios, there may be situations where custom permissions are needed. To create a custom permission level:

- Navigate to the site permissions settings (Site settings > Site permissions).

- Click on "Permission Levels."

- Click "Add a Permission Level."

- Define the permissions by selecting the appropriate checkboxes.

- Name the custom permission level and provide a description.

- Click "Create" to save the custom permission level.

- This custom level can now be assigned to users or groups in the list permissions settings.

Best Practices for Permissions Management

1. Principle of Least Privilege

To minimize security risks, always follow the principle of least privilege. This means granting users the minimum level of access they need to perform their tasks. Avoid assigning full control or edit permissions unless absolutely necessary.

2. Use Groups for Permissions

Instead of assigning permissions to individual users, use SharePoint groups. This simplifies permissions management, especially as team members join or leave the organization. By adding or removing users from groups, their permissions are automatically updated.

3. Regularly Review and Audit Permissions

Periodically review the permissions for your lists to ensure they are still appropriate. Remove access for users who no longer need it and adjust permissions as roles and responsibilities change. SharePoint's auditing capabilities can help track permission changes and identify any potential issues.

4. Document Permissions Policies

Establish and document your organization's permissions policies for Microsoft Lists and SharePoint. This should include guidelines on who can grant permissions, how permissions should be managed, and the process for requesting access changes. Clear policies help maintain consistency and security.

Permissions in Real-World Scenarios

1. Project Management Lists

In a project management scenario, different stakeholders may require varying levels of access. For instance:

- Project Managers: Full Control to create, edit, and delete tasks, milestones, and project documents.

- Team Members: Contribute permissions to update task status, add comments, and attach files.

- Clients or External Partners: Read permissions to view project progress and milestones without making any changes.

2. HR and Employee Data Lists

For HR-related lists containing sensitive employee information:

- HR Managers: Full Control to manage employee records, leave requests, and performance evaluations.

- Supervisors: Edit permissions to update employee performance data and leave approvals.

- Employees: Read permissions to view their own records, with item-level permissions set for personal data visibility.

3. Sales and Marketing Lists

In a sales and marketing context:

- Sales Managers: Full Control to manage sales leads, opportunities, and customer data.

- Sales Reps: Edit permissions to update lead status, add notes, and log activities.

- Marketing Team: Contribute permissions to add campaign data, track performance, and update marketing materials.

Advanced Permissions Techniques

1. Item-Level Permissions

In some scenarios, certain list items may contain highly sensitive data. To set item-level permissions:

- Select the item in the list.

- Click on the ellipsis (three dots) next to the item and select "Manage Permissions."

- Click "Stop Inheriting Permissions" to break the inheritance from the list.

- Grant or remove permissions as needed for the specific item.

2. Sharing Links with Specific Permissions

Microsoft Lists allows you to share links with specific permissions:

- Click the "Share" button for the list or item.

- Select "Anyone with the link" for broad access or "Specific people" for more control.

- Choose whether recipients can view or edit the content.

- Generate and share the link with the appropriate users.

3. External Sharing

When collaborating with external partners or clients, external sharing options are available:

- Enable external sharing at the SharePoint site level.

- Share the list or specific items with external users by entering their email addresses.

- External users will receive an invitation and may need to authenticate before accessing the content.

Conclusion

Effective permissions and access control are fundamental to leveraging the collaborative power of Microsoft Lists while ensuring data security and integrity. By understanding and implementing the appropriate permissions settings, organizations can foster teamwork, streamline workflows, and protect sensitive information. Regular reviews and adherence to best practices will help maintain a secure and efficient environment for all users.

Collaborating in Real-Time

Real-time collaboration is a key feature of Microsoft Lists that enhances teamwork, productivity, and efficiency. It allows multiple users to work on the same list simultaneously, making updates and changes visible to everyone in real-time. This section explores how to effectively collaborate in real-time using Microsoft Lists.

Introduction to Real-Time Collaboration

Real-time collaboration in Microsoft Lists is facilitated through seamless integration with other Microsoft 365 applications, especially Microsoft Teams. This integration provides a unified platform where team members can access, edit, and update lists without the need for constant back-and-forth communication. The changes are reflected instantly, ensuring that everyone is always working with the most up-to-date information.

Setting Up Real-Time Collaboration

To begin collaborating in real-time, you need to share your list with the relevant team members and ensure they have the necessary permissions. Here's a step-by-step guide:

1. Share the List: Navigate to the list you want to share. Click on the "Share" button at the top right corner of the screen. Enter the email addresses of the team members you want to share the list with. You can also generate a sharing link if you prefer to send the link directly.

2. Set Permissions: When sharing the list, you can specify the level of access each team member should have. Options include "Can Edit" and "Can View." For real-time collaboration, ensure that team members have "Can Edit" permissions.

3. Notify Team Members: After sharing the list, notify your team members via email or through a Microsoft Teams message. Provide them with the link to the list and any specific instructions or guidelines for collaboration.

Using Microsoft Teams for Enhanced Collaboration

Microsoft Teams enhances real-time collaboration by providing a centralized platform for communication and list management. Here's how to leverage Microsoft Teams for collaborating on Microsoft Lists:

1. Add the List to a Teams Channel: In Microsoft Teams, navigate to the channel where you want to collaborate on the list. Click on the "+" icon to add a new tab. Select "Lists" from the available options and choose the list you want to add. This integration allows team members to access and edit the list directly within Teams.

2. Communicate in Real-Time: Use the chat functionality in Teams to discuss updates, changes, and tasks related to the list. You can mention specific team members using the "@" symbol to draw their attention to important updates or questions.

3. Use Video and Voice Calls: For more complex discussions or to resolve issues quickly, initiate a video or voice call within Teams. This helps to clarify any misunderstandings and ensures that everyone is on the same page.

4. Collaborate on List Items: Team members can simultaneously work on different items in the list. For instance, one member can update the status of a task while another adds comments or attachments. All changes are saved and displayed in real-time.

Best Practices for Real-Time Collaboration

Effective real-time collaboration requires clear communication, defined roles, and proper management of the list. Here are some best practices to ensure smooth collaboration:

1. Define Roles and Responsibilities: Clearly define who is responsible for what within the list. Assign specific tasks to team members and ensure everyone knows their roles.

2. Communicate Regularly: Regular communication is essential for effective collaboration. Use Microsoft Teams to keep everyone informed about updates, changes, and deadlines.

3. Set Up Notifications: Enable notifications for changes to the list. This ensures that team members are promptly informed about updates and can respond quickly.

4. Use Comments and Mentions: Utilize the commenting feature to add notes or feedback to specific list items. Use mentions to notify relevant team members about important comments.

5. Track Changes and Version Control: Use the version control features in Microsoft Lists to track changes and view the history of updates. This helps in identifying who made changes and when, ensuring accountability and transparency.

Real-Time Collaboration Scenarios

Let's explore some practical scenarios where real-time collaboration in Microsoft Lists can significantly enhance productivity:

1. Project Management: In a project management scenario, team members can use a shared list to track tasks, deadlines, and progress. Real-time collaboration allows for immediate updates on task statuses, enabling project managers to monitor progress and address issues as they arise.

2. Event Planning: For event planning, a shared list can be used to manage tasks, schedules, and resources. Team members can update the list in real-time, ensuring that everyone is aware of the latest developments and can adjust their plans accordingly.

3. Customer Support: Customer support teams can use a shared list to track support tickets and their statuses. Real-time collaboration ensures that support agents have access to the most current information, allowing them to provide timely and accurate responses to customers.

4. Inventory Management: In an inventory management scenario, team members can use a shared list to update stock levels, record new inventory, and track shipments. Real-time updates help in maintaining accurate inventory records and ensuring that stock levels are always current.

Troubleshooting Real-Time Collaboration Issues

While real-time collaboration is powerful, it can sometimes encounter issues. Here are some common problems and their solutions:

1. Permission Issues: If team members are unable to edit the list, check their permissions. Ensure they have "Can Edit" access.

2. Synchronization Delays: If changes are not appearing in real-time, ensure that all team members have a stable internet connection. Refresh the list or Teams page to force synchronization.

3. Conflicts and Overwrites: When multiple users edit the same item simultaneously, conflicts may arise. Microsoft Lists usually handles this by saving the latest change, but it's good practice to communicate and avoid simultaneous edits on the same item.

4. Access Issues: If team members are unable to access the list, ensure that the sharing link is correct and they are logged into the correct Microsoft account.

Conclusion

Real-time collaboration in Microsoft Lists transforms how teams work together, making processes more efficient and organized. By leveraging the integration with Microsoft Teams and following best practices, teams can maximize the benefits of real-time collaboration. Whether managing projects, planning events, or handling customer support, Microsoft Lists provides the tools necessary for seamless and effective teamwork.

In the next section, we will explore how to use comments and mentions to enhance collaboration further, ensuring that communication is clear and effective within your lists.

4.2 Commenting and Mentions

Adding Comments to List Items

Introduction to Commenting in Microsoft Lists

Adding comments to list items in Microsoft Lists is a powerful feature that enhances collaboration and communication among team members. This feature allows users to provide feedback, ask questions, and discuss specific list items directly within the list itself, ensuring that all relevant information is stored in one place. In this section, we will explore the process of adding comments to list items, discuss best practices for effective commenting, and highlight the benefits of using comments for team collaboration.

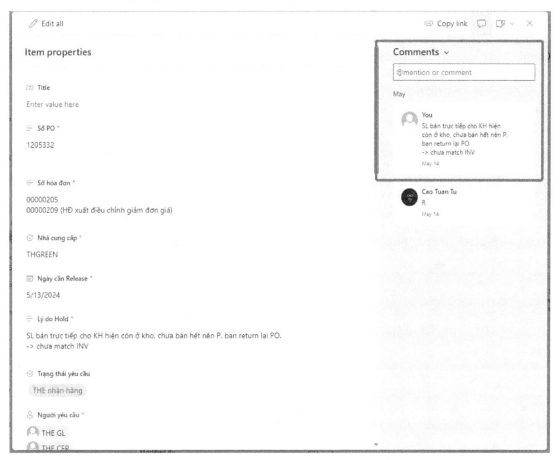

The Importance of Comments in Collaborative Work

Comments play a crucial role in collaborative work environments. They facilitate transparent communication, provide context to list items, and help keep track of discussions and decisions made about specific items. By using comments, team members can ensure that everyone involved in a project is on the same page, reducing misunderstandings and increasing efficiency.

How to Add Comments to List Items

Adding comments to list items in Microsoft Lists is a straightforward process. Follow these steps to add a comment to a list item:

1. Open the List: Navigate to the Microsoft Lists application and open the list that contains the item you want to comment on.

2. Select the Item: Click on the list item to open its detailed view. This action will display all the item's fields and associated metadata.

3. Access the Comments Pane: In the item's detailed view, locate the comments pane. This pane is usually found on the right side of the screen or at the bottom, depending on your interface settings.

4. Add Your Comment: Click on the comments pane to activate the text box. Type your comment in the text box provided. You can format your comment using basic text formatting options, such as bold, italic, and bullet points, to enhance clarity.

5. Post the Comment: Once you have written your comment, click the "Post" button to add it to the list item. Your comment will now be visible to all users who have access to the list.

Best Practices for Adding Comments

To make the most out of the commenting feature in Microsoft Lists, consider the following best practices:

1. Be Clear and Concise: When adding a comment, ensure that your message is clear and to the point. Avoid using jargon or ambiguous language that could lead to misunderstandings.

2. Provide Context: When commenting on a list item, provide sufficient context to help other users understand the purpose of your comment. Reference specific details or fields within the list item to clarify your message.

3. Use Formatting: Utilize basic text formatting options to highlight important points, create lists, or separate different sections of your comment. This will make your comment easier to read and understand.

4. Stay Professional: Maintain a professional tone when commenting on list items. Avoid using informal language or making personal remarks. Remember that comments are part of the official project documentation.

5. Encourage Feedback: Invite other team members to provide their input by asking questions or requesting feedback in your comments. This fosters a collaborative environment and encourages active participation.

Benefits of Using Comments in Microsoft Lists

Implementing the use of comments in Microsoft Lists offers several benefits for team collaboration and project management:

1. Enhanced Communication: Comments provide a direct communication channel within the list, allowing team members to discuss specific items without switching to other communication tools.

2. Centralized Information: All comments related to a list item are stored in one place, making it easy to review discussions and decisions. This centralization reduces the risk of losing important information.

3. Improved Accountability: Comments can be used to document feedback, decisions, and actions taken on list items. This creates a transparent record of the project's progress and enhances accountability.

4. Real-Time Collaboration: Comments are updated in real-time, enabling team members to collaborate and respond to each other's feedback instantly. This reduces delays and accelerates the decision-making process.

5. Contextual Discussions: By commenting directly on list items, discussions are kept relevant and focused on specific topics. This context-specific communication improves the quality of the collaboration.

Examples of Effective Comments

Here are a few examples of effective comments that illustrate the best practices discussed above:

1. Clear and Concise: "Please review the budget estimate for this project. The total cost seems higher than expected. Can we find areas to reduce expenses?"

2. Providing Context: "I noticed that the due date for this task is approaching. Are there any updates on the progress? We need to ensure it's completed by the end of the week."

3. Using Formatting: "Here are the key points from the meeting:

  - The design needs to be finalized by Friday.

  - We need to allocate more resources to the development team.

  - The client requested additional features."

4. Encouraging Feedback: "I've updated the project timeline based on our recent discussion. Please review and let me know if there are any concerns or adjustments needed."

5. Staying Professional: "Great job on the report! I have a few suggestions for improvement:

  - Add more detail to the introduction section.

  - Include a summary of key findings at the end.

  - Double-check the formatting for consistency."

Common Use Cases for Comments

Comments in Microsoft Lists can be used in various scenarios to improve collaboration and project management. Here are some common use cases:

1. Task Management: Team members can comment on tasks to provide updates, ask for clarifications, or request additional information. This keeps everyone informed about the task's status and any challenges encountered.

2. Project Planning: During the planning phase, stakeholders can use comments to discuss project requirements, timelines, and resource allocation. This ensures that all relevant input is considered before finalizing the plan.

3. Issue Tracking: Comments can be used to document issues, suggest solutions, and track the progress of resolving problems. This creates a clear record of the issue's history and the actions taken to address it.

4. Document Reviews: When reviewing documents or reports, team members can use comments to provide feedback, suggest revisions, and ask questions. This collaborative review process improves the quality of the final document.

5. Client Communication: Comments can be used to capture client feedback and requests directly within the list. This keeps client communication organized and ensures that all feedback is addressed appropriately.

Conclusion

Adding comments to list items in Microsoft Lists is a valuable feature that enhances collaboration, improves communication, and helps keep project-related discussions organized. By following best practices and leveraging the benefits of comments, teams can work more efficiently and effectively. Whether you are managing tasks, planning projects, tracking issues, reviewing documents, or communicating with clients, comments in Microsoft Lists provide a powerful tool to support your collaborative efforts.

Using Mentions for Team Collaboration

Mentions are a powerful feature in Microsoft Lists that can significantly enhance team collaboration. By using mentions, you can draw attention to specific team members within comments, ensuring that important updates or questions are directed to the right people. This feature helps streamline communication, reduces the likelihood of missed information, and fosters a collaborative environment where team members are engaged and informed. In this section, we will explore how to effectively use mentions in Microsoft Lists for team collaboration, including practical examples and best practices.

Understanding Mentions

Mentions in Microsoft Lists function similarly to those in other Microsoft 365 applications such as Teams and Outlook. When you mention a colleague by typing the "@" symbol followed by their name, they receive a notification that they have been mentioned. This notification directs them to the specific comment or list item where the mention occurred, allowing them to quickly respond or take action.

How to Use Mentions

To use mentions in Microsoft Lists:

1. Open the List Item:

   Navigate to the list item where you want to add a comment.

2. Add a Comment:

   Click on the comments section or icon to open the commenting interface.

3. Type the "@" Symbol:

   In the comment field, type the "@" symbol followed by the name of the person you want to mention. As you type, a dropdown list of matching names will appear.

4. Select the Person:

   Click on the name of the person you want to mention. Their name will appear highlighted in the comment field.

5. Complete the Comment:

   Finish typing your comment and click "Send" or "Post" to save it. The mentioned person will receive a notification.

Benefits of Using Mentions

Using mentions in Microsoft Lists offers several benefits:

1. Targeted Communication:

Mentions ensure that specific individuals are notified about relevant updates or questions, reducing the noise and ensuring that important messages reach the right people.

2. Increased Visibility:

Mentions increase the visibility of comments within list items, making it easier for team members to track discussions and actions related to their tasks.

3. Enhanced Collaboration:

By directing comments to specific team members, mentions foster a more collaborative environment where everyone knows their responsibilities and can contribute effectively.

4. Streamlined Workflow:

Mentions help streamline workflows by ensuring that team members are promptly notified about tasks that require their attention, leading to faster response times and more efficient project management.

Best Practices for Using Mentions

To maximize the effectiveness of mentions in Microsoft Lists, consider the following best practices:

1. Be Clear and Concise:

When mentioning someone, ensure that your comment is clear and concise. Provide enough context so that the mentioned person understands the purpose of the mention and what action is required.

2. Use Mentions Sparingly:

Avoid overusing mentions. Use them when you need to direct a comment to a specific person or when their input is crucial. Overusing mentions can lead to notification fatigue and reduce their effectiveness.

3. Combine Mentions with Action Items:

When mentioning someone, try to combine the mention with specific action items. For example, "@JohnDoe Please review the attached document by EOD and provide your feedback." This approach clarifies what is expected and by when.

4. Follow Up on Mentions:

If you do not receive a response to a mention within a reasonable timeframe, follow up with the person directly. This ensures that important tasks do not fall through the cracks.

5. Respect Privacy and Permissions:

Ensure that you respect privacy and permissions when using mentions. Only mention individuals who are relevant to the discussion and have the necessary access to view the list item.

Practical Examples of Using Mentions

Let's explore some practical examples of how mentions can be used effectively in Microsoft Lists:

Example 1: Task Assignment

- Scenario: You are managing a project list and need a team member to review a document.

- Comment: "@JaneSmith Please review the project proposal and provide your feedback by tomorrow."

- Outcome: Jane receives a notification and knows that she needs to review the proposal and provide feedback by the specified deadline.

Example 2: Requesting Updates

- Scenario: You are tracking the progress of a task and need an update from the responsible team member.

- Comment: "@JohnDoe Can you please provide an update on the status of the client meeting preparations?"

- Outcome: John receives a notification and provides an update on the meeting preparations.

Example 3: Highlighting Issues

- Scenario: You have identified an issue with a list item and need input from a team member.

- Comment: "@AlexBrown I've noticed a discrepancy in the sales figures for Q2. Can you take a look and confirm?"

- Outcome: Alex receives a notification and investigates the discrepancy in the sales figures.

Example 4: Collaborating on Ideas

- Scenario: You are brainstorming ideas for a new project and want input from the team.

- Comment: "@Team I'd like to hear your thoughts on the new marketing strategy. Please share your ideas and suggestions."

- Outcome: All team members receive a notification and contribute their ideas to the discussion.

Managing Notifications

Effective use of mentions requires managing notifications to ensure that team members are not overwhelmed. Here are some tips for managing notifications:

1. Customize Notification Settings:

   Team members can customize their notification settings in Microsoft Lists to control how and when they receive notifications. This can include turning off unnecessary notifications or setting specific rules for mentions.

2. Use Email Notifications:

   In addition to in-app notifications, mentions can also trigger email notifications. Ensure that team members have their email notifications set up correctly so they do not miss important mentions.

3. Regularly Check Notifications:

   Encourage team members to regularly check their notifications in Microsoft Lists to stay up-to-date with mentions and comments. This ensures that they do not miss any important updates or action items.

4. Notification Summary:

   Microsoft Lists can provide a summary of notifications, making it easier for team members to review all mentions and comments at a glance. This feature helps in managing and prioritizing notifications effectively.

Conclusion

Mentions are a versatile and powerful feature in Microsoft Lists that can significantly enhance team collaboration. By using mentions effectively, you can ensure that important information reaches the right people, streamline communication, and foster a collaborative environment. Remember to use mentions judiciously, provide clear and concise comments, and manage notifications to maximize their impact.

Incorporating these practices into your daily workflow will help you and your team stay organized, informed, and productive. As you continue to use Microsoft Lists, you will discover even more ways to leverage mentions for efficient and effective collaboration.

4.3 Tracking Changes and Activity

Viewing List History

Introduction to List History

In any collaborative environment, tracking changes and understanding the historical context of your data is crucial. Microsoft Lists provides robust features for viewing list history, which allows you to see who made changes, what changes were made, and when they were made. This functionality is essential for maintaining data integrity, auditing changes, and ensuring accountability within your team.

Why Viewing List History is Important

Viewing list history offers several benefits:

- Accountability: Knowing who made specific changes ensures that team members are accountable for their actions.

- Transparency: Provides a clear record of modifications, helping to avoid misunderstandings or disputes.

- Audit Trail: Useful for compliance and regulatory requirements, ensuring that you have a clear record of all changes.

- Data Recovery: Enables the ability to revert to previous versions if incorrect data is entered.

Accessing List History

To view the history of a list in Microsoft Lists, follow these steps:

1. Open Your List: Navigate to the list for which you want to view the history.

2. Select an Item: Click on the item you are interested in to open its details pane.

3. View Version History: In the details pane, look for the "Version history" link or button. Clicking this will display a list of all changes made to the item.

Detailed Steps for Viewing Version History

1. Navigate to Your List: Open Microsoft Lists and select the list that contains the item you want to investigate.

2. Select the Item: Click on the item to highlight it, then click on the ellipsis (...) or right-click to open the context menu.

3. Open Version History: From the context menu, select "Version history." This action will open a new pane or window displaying all versions of the item.

4. Review the Changes: Each entry in the version history includes details such as the date and time of the change, the user who made the change, and a description of what was changed.

5. Compare Versions: If necessary, you can compare different versions to understand the specific changes made between them.

Understanding the Version History Interface

The version history interface in Microsoft Lists is designed to be user-friendly and informative. Here are some key elements you will encounter:

- Version Number: Each change is assigned a unique version number, with the most recent changes having higher numbers.

- Modified Date: The date and time when the change was made.

- Modified By: The user who made the change.

- Comments: If the user added comments when saving the change, these will be displayed here.

- Changes Made: A summary or list of the specific fields that were modified and their new values.

Practical Use Cases for Viewing List History

1. Error Correction

- If incorrect data is entered, you can identify when the error occurred and who made it. This allows for quick correction and communication with the responsible team member.

2. Audit and Compliance

- For organizations that must adhere to strict audit and compliance regulations, maintaining a detailed history of data changes is essential. Microsoft Lists provides the necessary transparency and record-keeping.

3. Team Collaboration

- When multiple team members work on the same list, understanding the history of changes helps avoid duplications and ensures everyone is on the same page.

4. Project Tracking

- In project management scenarios, keeping track of changes to task lists, schedules, and other critical information is crucial for project success.

Best Practices for Using Version History

1. Regularly Review Changes

- Make it a habit to regularly review the version history of critical lists to ensure data accuracy and integrity.

2. Encourage Commenting

- When making significant changes, encourage team members to add comments. This practice helps others understand the context and reason for changes.

3. Train Your Team

- Ensure that all team members are trained on how to access and interpret version history. This training promotes accountability and transparency.

4. Use Permissions Wisely

- Set appropriate permissions to ensure that only authorized users can make changes to critical lists. This practice reduces the risk of unauthorized modifications.

Limitations and Considerations

While viewing list history in Microsoft Lists is a powerful feature, it does come with some limitations and considerations:

- Storage Limitations: Depending on your organization's storage policies, the amount of historical data retained may be limited.

- Access Control: Ensure that only authorized personnel have access to version history to prevent misuse of information.

- Data Sensitivity: Be mindful of sensitive data and ensure that version history does not expose confidential information.

Conclusion

Viewing list history is an indispensable feature in Microsoft Lists that enhances accountability, transparency, and data integrity within your team. By understanding how to access and interpret version history, you can maintain a clear record of all changes, ensuring that your data remains accurate and reliable. Regularly reviewing version history and following best practices will help you make the most of this powerful tool, ultimately leading to more efficient and effective collaboration.

Using Version Control

Introduction to Version Control in Microsoft Lists

Version control is a fundamental feature in Microsoft Lists that allows users to track changes, maintain historical data, and ensure data integrity. It provides a way to monitor every change made to list items, enabling users to revert to previous versions if necessary. This is particularly useful in collaborative environments where multiple users may be editing the same list.

Version control helps in maintaining a record of all modifications, ensuring that changes are traceable and recoverable. This capability is essential for auditing purposes, maintaining data accuracy, and ensuring compliance with organizational policies.

Enabling Version Control

Before you can start using version control, it must be enabled on your list. Here's how you can do it:

1. Navigate to List Settings: Go to your Microsoft List and click on the settings gear icon in the top-right corner. Select "List settings" from the dropdown menu.

2. Versioning Settings: In the List Settings page, under the "General Settings" section, click on "Versioning settings."

3. Configure Versioning: On the Versioning Settings page, you can configure the following options:

   - Content Approval: This option allows you to require content approval for submitted items. This is useful for lists that require a review process before changes are published.

   - Create a Version Each Time You Edit an Item in This List: Enable this option to create a new version each time an item is edited. You can also specify the number of versions to retain.

   - Require Check Out: This option forces users to check out an item before editing it, which can help prevent conflicts and ensure that only one user edits an item at a time.

Once you have configured these settings, click "OK" to save your changes.

Viewing and Managing Versions

After enabling version control, you can view and manage the versions of list items. Here's how you can do this:

1. Access the List Item: Open the list and click on the item for which you want to view the version history.

2. Version History: Click on the ellipsis (...) next to the item and select "Version history" from the menu. This will open a window displaying all the versions of the selected item.

3. Review Versions: In the Version History window, you can see details about each version, including the date and time of the change, the user who made the change, and any comments associated with the change.

4. Restore a Previous Version: If you need to revert to a previous version, select the version you want to restore and click on "Restore." This will make the selected version the current version of the item.

5. Delete Versions: You can also delete older versions if they are no longer needed. This can help manage storage and maintain a clean version history.

Best Practices for Using Version Control

To make the most out of version control in Microsoft Lists, consider the following best practices:

1. Regular Monitoring: Regularly monitor the version history of critical list items to ensure that changes are tracked and reviewed.

2. Clear Comments: Encourage users to add clear and descriptive comments when making changes. This can help provide context for each version and make it easier to understand the changes.

3. Set Retention Policies: Configure retention policies to automatically manage the number of versions stored. This can help prevent the version history from becoming cluttered and manage storage effectively.

4. Training and Awareness: Provide training to users on how to use version control effectively. Ensure that they understand the importance of checking out items and adding comments during edits.

5. Regular Audits: Conduct regular audits of version histories for key lists to ensure compliance with organizational policies and identify any potential issues.

Real-World Use Cases of Version Control

Use Case 1: Project Management

In project management, multiple team members often collaborate on lists that track tasks, milestones, and deliverables. Version control ensures that all changes to these lists are recorded, allowing project managers to review progress and make informed decisions. For example, if a task's status is updated from "In Progress" to "Completed," the version history will show when the change was made and by whom. This can help project managers track the completion of tasks and identify any delays.

Use Case 2: Quality Assurance

In quality assurance processes, maintaining accurate records of inspections, tests, and audits is crucial. Version control allows QA teams to track changes to inspection lists and ensure that all modifications are documented. If an inspection result is updated, the version history provides a detailed record of the change, including the reason for the update and the user who made it. This can help in maintaining data integrity and ensuring compliance with industry standards.

Use Case 3: Human Resources

In HR, version control can be used to manage employee records, performance reviews, and training logs. For example, if an employee's performance review is updated, the version history will show the changes made to the review, including comments and ratings. This can help HR managers track employee performance over time and ensure that records are accurate and up-to-date.

Use Case 4: Legal and Compliance

In legal and compliance functions, maintaining accurate records is essential for audits and regulatory requirements. Version control ensures that all changes to compliance-related lists are recorded and traceable. For example, if a compliance checklist is updated, the version history will provide a detailed record of the changes, including the date, time, and user who made the update. This can help organizations demonstrate compliance with regulations and prepare for audits.

Advanced Features of Version Control

Minor and Major Versions:

Microsoft Lists supports both minor and major versions, providing additional flexibility in version control. Minor versions are typically used for drafts and intermediate changes, while major versions are used for final or significant changes.

- Enabling Minor Versions: To enable minor versions, go to the Versioning Settings page and select the option to create minor versions. You can specify the number of minor versions to retain.

- Managing Minor Versions: When editing an item, you can choose to save it as a minor version. This is useful for ongoing work that is not yet ready for a major version release.

Draft Item Security

Draft item security allows you to control who can see minor versions of list items. This is useful for controlling access to work-in-progress changes and ensuring that only authorized users can view draft versions.

- Configuring Draft Item Security: In the Versioning Settings page, you can configure draft item security settings. You can choose to restrict access to draft versions to only users who can edit items or only users who can approve items.

Using Check-Out and Check-In

Check-out and check-in functionality helps prevent conflicts when multiple users are editing the same list item. When an item is checked out, it is locked for editing by the user who checked it out.

- Checking Out an Item: To check out an item, click on the ellipsis (...) next to the item and select "Check out." The item is now locked for editing by you.

- Checking In an Item: After making your changes, check in the item by selecting "Check in" from the same menu. You can add comments about the changes made during the check-out period.

Auditing and Compliance

Version control plays a crucial role in auditing and compliance. It provides a detailed record of all changes made to list items, helping organizations demonstrate compliance with internal policies and external regulations.

- Audit Logs: Microsoft Lists integrates with Microsoft 365's auditing features, allowing you to generate audit logs that include details about changes to list items. This can help in preparing for audits and maintaining compliance.

- Compliance Policies: You can configure compliance policies to automatically manage version histories and ensure that records are retained according to regulatory requirements.

Conclusion

Version control is an essential feature in Microsoft Lists that enhances data management, collaboration, and compliance. By enabling version control, users can track changes, maintain historical data, and ensure data integrity. Implementing best practices for version control, such as regular monitoring, clear comments, and retention policies, can help organizations make the most of this powerful feature.

Whether you are managing project tasks, conducting quality assurance, maintaining employee records, or ensuring compliance, version control in Microsoft Lists provides the tools you need to track changes and maintain accurate records. By leveraging advanced features such as minor and major versions, draft item security, and check-out/check-in functionality, you can further enhance your version control processes and ensure that your data is well-managed and compliant.

In summary, version control in Microsoft Lists is a critical component for effective data management and collaboration. By understanding and utilizing its features, you can ensure that your lists are organized, changes are traceable, and data integrity is maintained. This not only improves productivity and collaboration but also helps organizations meet their compliance and auditing requirements.

CHAPTER V
Managing Data in Microsoft Lists

5.1 Importing and Exporting Data

Importing Data from Excel and Other Sources

Importing data into Microsoft Lists is a fundamental task that allows users to bring in existing information from various sources, facilitating a seamless transition to a more organized and collaborative environment. This section will guide you through the process of importing data from Excel and other sources into Microsoft Lists, providing step-by-step instructions, tips, and best practices to ensure a smooth and efficient data import process.

1. Understanding the Importance of Data Importing

Data importing is essential for several reasons:

- Efficiency: It saves time by allowing you to utilize existing data without manual entry.

- Consistency: It ensures that data remains consistent across different platforms.

- Accuracy: It minimizes errors that can occur during manual data entry.

- Collaboration: It facilitates collaboration by making data accessible to team members within Microsoft Lists.

2. Preparing Your Data for Import

Before importing data, it's crucial to prepare your data to ensure a successful import:

- Data Cleanliness: Ensure your data is clean and free of errors. Remove duplicates, correct inconsistencies, and validate the data.

- Format Consistency: Ensure that the data format in your source file matches the expected format in Microsoft Lists. For example, dates should be in a recognizable format, and numeric data should be consistently formatted.

- Column Headers: Ensure that your source data includes column headers. These headers will be used to create corresponding columns in your Microsoft List.

- Data Completeness: Ensure that all necessary data is present and complete. Missing data can cause issues during the import process.

3. Importing Data from Excel

Excel is one of the most common sources for importing data into Microsoft Lists. Follow these steps to import data from an Excel file:

Step 1: Prepare Your Excel File

- Open your Excel file and ensure that the data is formatted correctly. Each column should have a header, and the data should be organized in rows beneath these headers.

- Save the Excel file in a compatible format, such as .xlsx or .xls.

Step 2: Access Microsoft Lists

- Navigate to the Microsoft Lists app from your Microsoft 365 portal. You can also access Lists from within Microsoft Teams or SharePoint.

Step 3: Create a New List from Excel

- Click on the "+ New list" button.

- Select the "From Excel" option. This will prompt you to upload your Excel file.

Step 4: Upload Your Excel File

- Click the "Upload file" button and select your prepared Excel file.

- Microsoft Lists will automatically read the data from your Excel file and display a preview.

Step 5: Map Excel Columns to List Columns

- Review the column mapping in the preview. Microsoft Lists will attempt to map Excel columns to list columns based on the headers.

- You can adjust the column types and names if necessary. For example, you might want to change a column type from "Single line of text" to "Number" or "Date".

Step 6: Finalize the Import

- Click the "Create" button to finalize the import process.

- Your data will be imported into a new list, with each row in the Excel file becoming an item in the list.

4. Importing Data from Other Sources

In addition to Excel, you can import data from other sources, such as CSV files, SharePoint lists, and other databases.

Importing from CSV Files

- Prepare Your CSV File: Ensure that your CSV file is properly formatted, with column headers and consistent data.

- Upload and Map Columns: Follow a similar process to the Excel import, uploading your CSV file and mapping the columns.

Importing from SharePoint Lists

- Export to Excel: If your data is in a SharePoint list, you can export the list to Excel and then import it into Microsoft Lists.

- Direct Import: In some cases, you might be able to directly import data from a SharePoint list by using Power Automate to create flows that move data between SharePoint and Microsoft Lists.

Importing from Databases

- Export Data: Export the data from your database into a CSV or Excel format.

- Use Power Query: Utilize Power Query in Excel to connect to databases and fetch data directly, which can then be imported into Microsoft Lists.

5. Best Practices for Data Importing

To ensure a successful data import, follow these best practices:

- Validate Data: Always validate your data before importing to catch any errors or inconsistencies.

- Backup Data: Keep a backup of your original data in case something goes wrong during the import process.

- Test Import: Perform a test import with a small subset of data to ensure that the import process works correctly.

- Documentation: Document the import process, including any mappings or transformations, for future reference and repeatability.

6. Troubleshooting Common Issues

Despite careful preparation, you might encounter issues during the import process. Here are some common problems and solutions:

- Incorrect Data Types: If data types are incorrectly mapped, adjust the column types during the import process.

- Missing Data: Ensure that all required data is present in the source file. Missing data can cause import failures.

- Duplicate Entries: Clean your data to remove duplicates before importing.

- Large Data Sets: For very large data sets, consider breaking the data into smaller chunks and importing them separately.

7. Automating Data Imports

For regular data imports, consider automating the process using Power Automate:

- Create Flows: Use Power Automate to create flows that automatically import data from various sources into Microsoft Lists.

- Scheduled Imports: Schedule regular data imports to keep your lists up to date.

Conclusion

Importing data from Excel and other sources into Microsoft Lists is a powerful way to streamline your workflow and ensure that your data is organized and accessible. By following the steps and best practices outlined in this section, you can efficiently import data and take full advantage of Microsoft Lists' capabilities to manage and collaborate on your data. Whether you are importing data from Excel, CSV files, SharePoint lists, or databases, the key is to prepare your data carefully and follow a structured import process to ensure success.

Exporting Lists to Excel and CSV

Exporting data from Microsoft Lists to Excel and CSV formats is an essential feature that allows users to share, analyze, and manipulate their data using powerful spreadsheet tools. This section will cover the step-by-step process of exporting data, the benefits of doing so, and practical tips to maximize the use of exported data.

Overview of Exporting Data

Exporting data from Microsoft Lists is a straightforward process that enables you to move your list data into other applications like Microsoft Excel or any software that supports CSV (Comma-Separated Values) format. This capability is particularly useful for:

1. Data Analysis: Use Excel's advanced data analysis tools to perform complex calculations, create pivot tables, and generate charts.

2. Data Sharing: Share data with stakeholders who may not have access to Microsoft Lists but can work with Excel or CSV files.

3. Data Backup: Keep a backup of your data in a universal format that can be accessed even if your access to Microsoft Lists is disrupted.

Exporting Lists to Excel

Excel is a versatile tool that integrates seamlessly with Microsoft Lists. Here's how to export your list data to an Excel file:

1. Access Your List:

  - Open Microsoft Lists and navigate to the list you want to export.

  - Ensure that the data is up-to-date and that you have the necessary permissions to export the list.

2. Initiate the Export:

  - Click on the "Export" button, usually located in the toolbar at the top of the list interface.

  - Select "Export to Excel" from the dropdown menu.

3. Download the File:

  - A download prompt will appear. Click "Download" to save the file to your local machine.

  - The file will be saved as an `.xlsx` file, which can be opened using Microsoft Excel or any other compatible spreadsheet application.

4. Open and Review in Excel:

  - Open the downloaded Excel file. The data from your list will be displayed in a table format.

  - Review the data to ensure it has been exported correctly. The columns and rows should match the structure of your list.

Customizing Exported Data

Before exporting, you might want to customize the data to ensure it meets your needs. This can involve filtering and sorting the data within Microsoft Lists:

1. Filtering Data:

  - Use the filter options within Microsoft Lists to display only the data you want to export. For example, you can filter by date, status, or any other column criteria.

  - This is useful if you only need a subset of the data for analysis or reporting.

2. Sorting Data:

- Sort the list data by one or more columns to organize it in a meaningful way before exporting.

- For instance, you might sort by date to ensure the data is in chronological order.

3. Custom Views:

- Create custom views in Microsoft Lists to display specific columns and data points. This way, only the relevant data will be included in the export.

- Navigate to the view settings and customize the columns and filters according to your requirements.

Exporting Lists to CSV

The CSV format is widely used for data interchange because it is simple and compatible with many applications. Here's how to export your list data to a CSV file:

1. Access Your List:

- Open Microsoft Lists and navigate to the list you want to export.

- Ensure that the data is up-to-date and that you have the necessary permissions to export the list.

2. Initiate the Export:

- Click on the "Export" button, usually located in the toolbar at the top of the list interface.

- Select "Export to CSV" from the dropdown menu.

3. Download the File:

- A download prompt will appear. Click "Download" to save the file to your local machine.

- The file will be saved as a `.csv` file, which can be opened using any text editor, spreadsheet software, or imported into databases and other applications.

4. Open and Review in a CSV-Compatible Application:

- Open the downloaded CSV file in a text editor (such as Notepad) or spreadsheet software (such as Excel).

- Review the data to ensure it has been exported correctly. Each line in the CSV file represents a row in your list, and each field is separated by a comma.

Tips for Working with Exported Data

Once you have exported your data, there are several best practices to consider:

1. Data Integrity:

  - Check for any discrepancies or missing data in the exported file.

  - Ensure that all columns and rows from the list are correctly represented in the export.

2. Data Cleaning:

  - Before analyzing the data, clean it to remove any inconsistencies, duplicates, or irrelevant information.

  - Use Excel's data cleaning tools or write scripts if you are working with a large dataset.

3. Data Analysis:

  - Utilize Excel's powerful analysis features such as pivot tables, charts, and conditional formatting to derive insights from your data.

  - Create reports and dashboards to visualize the data and share insights with stakeholders.

4. Data Backup and Security:

  - Store your exported files securely, especially if they contain sensitive information.

  - Consider encrypting the files or storing them in a secure location to prevent unauthorized access.

5. Automation:

  - If you frequently export data, consider automating the process using Power Automate or other automation tools.

  - Set up workflows that automatically export and email the data at regular intervals.

Practical Example: Exporting and Analyzing Sales Data

Let's walk through a practical example of exporting and analyzing sales data:

1. Scenario:

  - You have a sales list in Microsoft Lists that tracks monthly sales data, including sales amount, date, salesperson, and product category.

2. Filtering and Customizing:

  - Before exporting, you filter the list to show sales data for the last quarter.

  - You create a custom view that only includes columns for date, salesperson, and sales amount.

3. Exporting to Excel:

  - You initiate the export process and download the filtered data as an Excel file.

  - Open the Excel file and review the data to ensure accuracy.

4. Analyzing in Excel:

  - Use Excel's pivot table feature to summarize sales data by salesperson and product category.

  - Create charts to visualize sales trends over the quarter.

5. Sharing Insights:

  - Generate a sales report in Excel that includes pivot tables, charts, and key insights.

  - Share the report with your team and stakeholders to inform business decisions.

Conclusion

Exporting data from Microsoft Lists to Excel and CSV formats is a powerful feature that enhances your ability to analyze, share, and utilize your data effectively. By following the steps outlined in this section and applying best practices, you can ensure a smooth and efficient export process. Whether you are a beginner or an advanced user, understanding how to export and work with your data will significantly improve your productivity and data management capabilities.

5.2 Data Validation and Formatting

Setting Up Data Validation Rules

Data validation is a crucial feature in Microsoft Lists that ensures data accuracy and consistency. By setting up data validation rules, you can control the type of data entered into your lists, prevent errors, and maintain the integrity of your information. This section will guide you through the process of setting up data validation rules in Microsoft Lists, providing practical examples and best practices.

Understanding Data Validation in Microsoft Lists

Data validation involves defining constraints or conditions that data must meet to be accepted into a list. These constraints help in maintaining data quality by ensuring that only valid data is entered. For example, you can set rules to ensure that dates are entered in a specific format, numerical values fall within a certain range, or text entries match a predefined list of options.

Benefits of Data Validation

1. Consistency: Data validation ensures that data is consistent across the list, making it easier to analyze and report.

2. Accuracy: It reduces the risk of errors by preventing invalid data entries.

3. Compliance: Helps in complying with data standards and regulations.

4. Efficiency: Saves time by minimizing the need for data cleaning and corrections.

Steps to Set Up Data Validation Rules

1. Identify the Data to Validate:

   - Determine which columns require validation. Common columns that benefit from validation include dates, numbers, email addresses, and choice fields.

2. Access List Settings:

  - Navigate to your Microsoft List and click on the settings gear icon at the top right corner.

  - Select "List settings" from the dropdown menu.

3. Choose the Column to Validate:

  - In the List Settings page, scroll down to the "Columns" section.

  - Click on the column name you want to set up validation for.

4. Define Validation Criteria:

  - In the column settings, look for the "Column Validation" section.

  - Here, you can define the validation criteria using formulas and expressions.

Types of Validation Rules

1. Text Validation:

  - Example: Ensure that a text entry matches a specific format or contains certain keywords.

  - Formula: `=AND(LEN([Column Name]) > 0, ISNUMBER(FIND("keyword", [Column Name])))`

  - Description: This rule ensures that the text entry is not empty and contains the word "keyword."

2. Number Validation:

  - Example: Ensure that a numerical value falls within a specified range.

  - Formula: `=AND([Column Name] >= 10, [Column Name] <= 100)`

  - Description: This rule ensures that the value entered is between 10 and 100.

3. Date Validation:

  - Example: Ensure that the date entered is within a specific timeframe.

  - Formula: `=AND([Column Name] >= [Start Date], [Column Name] <= [End Date])`

- Description: This rule ensures that the date is between the specified start and end dates.

4. Choice Field Validation:

   - Example: Ensure that the entry matches one of the predefined choices.

   - Formula: `=OR([Column Name] = "Choice1", [Column Name] = "Choice2", [Column Name] = "Choice3")`

   - Description: This rule ensures that the entry matches one of the specified choices.

Practical Examples

1. Email Address Validation:

   - Formula: `=AND(ISNUMBER(FIND("@", [Email Column])), ISNUMBER(FIND(".", [Email Column])))`

   - Description: This rule ensures that the email address contains both "@" and "." symbols.

2. Phone Number Validation:

   - Formula: `=AND(ISNUMBER([Phone Column]), LEN([Phone Column]) = 10)`

   - Description: This rule ensures that the phone number is a 10-digit number.

3. Custom Text Pattern Validation:

   - Example: Ensure that a product code follows the format "PROD-XXXX" where "X" is a digit.

   - Formula: `=AND(LEFT([Product Code], 5) = "PROD-", ISNUMBER(VALUE(MID([Product Code], 6, 4))))`

   - Description: This rule ensures that the product code starts with "PROD-" and is followed by four digits.

Implementing and Testing Validation Rules

Once you have defined the validation rules, it's essential to test them to ensure they work as expected. Here's how to implement and test your validation rules:

1. Save the Column Settings:

- After defining the validation formula, click "OK" or "Save" to apply the changes.

2. Test Data Entry:

 - Go back to your list and try entering data into the column with the validation rule.

 - Ensure that the rule prevents invalid entries and accepts valid ones.

3. Adjust and Refine:

 - If the validation rule does not work as expected, revisit the column settings and adjust the formula.

 - Test the rule again after making adjustments.

Best Practices for Data Validation

1. Keep Rules Simple:

 - Start with simple validation rules and gradually add complexity if needed. Complex rules can be harder to debug and maintain.

2. Provide Clear Error Messages:

 - When setting up validation, provide clear and concise error messages to guide users on what is expected. This helps in reducing frustration and improving data entry accuracy.

3. Use Consistent Validation Across Lists:

 - Apply similar validation rules across multiple lists where applicable to maintain consistency and standardization.

4. Regularly Review and Update Rules:

 - Periodically review and update validation rules to ensure they remain relevant and effective as data requirements evolve.

Common Scenarios for Data Validation

1. Project Management:

 - Ensuring task dates are within project timelines.

- Validating status updates to predefined categories.

2. Sales and Marketing:

  - Validating lead information such as email addresses and phone numbers.

  - Ensuring sales figures are within realistic ranges.

3. Human Resources:

  - Validating employee IDs and ensuring no duplicates.

  - Ensuring data entry for mandatory fields like joining date and department.

Conclusion

Setting up data validation rules in Microsoft Lists is a powerful way to ensure data quality, accuracy, and consistency. By defining appropriate validation criteria, you can prevent errors, save time on data cleaning, and improve the reliability of your lists. Use the steps and examples provided in this section to implement effective data validation in your Microsoft Lists, and follow best practices to maintain a high standard of data integrity.

Customizing Data Formatting

Introduction to Data Formatting

Data formatting is an essential aspect of managing data within Microsoft Lists. It enhances readability, highlights important information, and ensures consistency across the list. Customizing data formatting allows users to visually differentiate data, making it easier to interpret and analyze. In this section, we will delve into various techniques and best practices for customizing data formatting in Microsoft Lists.

Understanding Data Formatting Options

Microsoft Lists offers a range of data formatting options that can be applied to different data types. These options include text formatting, conditional formatting, and advanced formatting using JSON. Each of these methods serves a unique purpose and can be combined to achieve the desired outcome.

1. Text Formatting

Text formatting is the most basic form of data formatting. It involves adjusting the appearance of text within list items, such as changing font styles, sizes, and colors. Text formatting can be applied to columns to make them more visually appealing and easier to read.

- Font Styles and Sizes: Users can change the font style and size to enhance the readability of list items. For example, increasing the font size of important columns can draw attention to critical information.

- Font Colors: Applying different font colors can help distinguish between different types of data. For instance, using green for positive values and red for negative values can provide immediate visual cues.

2. Conditional Formatting

Conditional formatting allows users to apply specific formatting rules based on the data within the list. This dynamic approach to formatting makes it possible to highlight data that meets certain criteria, thereby improving data analysis and decision-making.

- Highlighting Important Data: Conditional formatting can be used to highlight important data, such as deadlines, high-priority tasks, or items that require immediate attention. For example, overdue tasks can be highlighted in red to make them stand out.

- Color Scales: Color scales use a gradient of colors to represent a range of values. This is particularly useful for numerical data, as it provides a visual representation of variations within the data. For example, a color scale from green to red can indicate performance levels, with green representing high performance and red representing low performance.

3. Advanced Formatting with JSON

For more complex formatting requirements, Microsoft Lists supports advanced formatting using JSON (JavaScript Object Notation). JSON formatting allows users to customize the appearance of list items beyond the standard options provided by the user interface.

- Custom Display Templates: JSON can be used to create custom display templates for list items. This includes changing the layout of list items, adding icons, and incorporating custom styles. For example, a custom template can be created to display task status with different icons for "Completed," "In Progress," and "Not Started."

- Conditional Logic: JSON formatting can incorporate conditional logic to apply different formatting based on specific conditions. For instance, a rule can be created to display different background colors for list items based on their status or priority level.

Step-by-Step Guide to Customizing Data Formatting

Customizing data formatting in Microsoft Lists involves a series of steps. Here, we provide a detailed guide to help users apply various formatting techniques effectively.

1. Accessing the Column Settings

   To customize data formatting, users need to access the column settings within the list.

   - Navigate to the list you want to format.

   - Click on the column header you wish to format.

   - Select "Column settings" from the dropdown menu.

   - Choose "Format this column" to open the formatting panel.

2. Applying Text Formatting

   Text formatting can be applied directly from the formatting panel.

   - In the formatting panel, select the desired text formatting options, such as font style, size, and color.

   - Apply the changes to see the updated appearance of the list items.

3. Setting Up Conditional Formatting

Conditional formatting involves creating rules based on specific criteria.

- In the formatting panel, select "Conditional formatting."

- Click "Add a rule" to create a new formatting rule.

- Define the criteria for the rule. For example, to highlight overdue tasks, set the condition to "Due Date is before today."

- Choose the formatting options for items that meet the criteria, such as changing the background color to red.

- Apply the rule to see the changes in the list.

4. Using JSON for Advanced Formatting

For more advanced formatting, users can use JSON.

- In the formatting panel, select "Advanced mode."

- Enter the JSON code to define the custom formatting. Microsoft provides documentation and templates to help users get started with JSON formatting.

- Save the changes to apply the custom formatting to the list.

Best Practices for Data Formatting

To ensure effective data formatting, users should follow these best practices:

1. Consistency: Maintain consistency in formatting across different lists and columns. Consistent formatting helps users quickly understand and interpret data.

2. Simplicity: Avoid overly complex formatting that can make the list difficult to read. Simple, clear formatting is more effective in highlighting important information.

3. Accessibility: Consider accessibility when applying formatting. Ensure that color choices and font styles are accessible to all users, including those with visual impairments.

4. Testing: Test formatting changes to ensure they display correctly and achieve the desired effect. This is especially important when using advanced JSON formatting.

Examples of Custom Data Formatting

To illustrate the application of data formatting, here are some practical examples:

1. Highlighting Urgent Tasks

   - Create a conditional formatting rule to highlight tasks with a due date within the next three days.

   - Set the background color to yellow for these tasks to draw attention.

2. Visualizing Task Status

   - Use JSON to create custom display templates for task status.

   - Display "Completed" tasks with a green checkmark icon, "In Progress" tasks with a blue circle, and "Not Started" tasks with a red cross.

3. Applying Color Scales to Performance Data

   - Use color scales to represent performance data in a list.

   - Apply a gradient from green (high performance) to red (low performance) to visualize variations in performance levels.

Conclusion

Customizing data formatting in Microsoft Lists is a powerful way to enhance data presentation and usability. By applying text formatting, conditional formatting, and advanced JSON techniques, users can create visually appealing and informative lists that improve data analysis and decision-making. Following best practices ensures that formatting is effective, accessible, and consistent, ultimately leading to better organization and productivity.

5.3 Using Calculated Columns

Creating Formulas in Lists

Calculated columns in Microsoft Lists allow you to perform dynamic calculations on your list data. This feature is incredibly powerful, providing the capability to automate data processing, enhance data integrity, and generate meaningful insights without the need for external tools. In this section, we will delve into the process of creating formulas in calculated columns, understand the syntax and functions available, and explore practical examples to illustrate their application.

Understanding Calculated Columns

A calculated column is a special type of column where the value is derived from a formula. This formula can use values from other columns in the same list, and it can include functions, operators, and constants. Calculated columns are updated automatically whenever the data in the list changes, ensuring that your calculations are always up to date.

Creating a Calculated Column

To create a calculated column, follow these steps:

1. Open Your List: Navigate to the Microsoft List you want to work with.

2. Add a New Column: Click on the "+ Add column" button on the right side of your list header.

3. Select Calculated: From the list of column types, select "Calculated."

4. Configure the Column: In the configuration panel, you will need to provide the following details:

   - Column Name: Enter a name for your calculated column.

   - Formula: This is where you will enter the formula for your calculation.

   - Data Type: Specify the data type of the result (e.g., single line of text, number, date and time).

5. Save: Click "Save" to create the column.

Writing Formulas

Formulas in Microsoft Lists are similar to those used in Excel. They start with an equals sign (`=`) and can include functions, references to other columns, operators, and constants. Here are some basic examples:

- Addition: `=[Column1] + [Column2]`

- Subtraction: `=[Column1] - [Column2]`

- Multiplication: `=[Column1]  [Column2]`

- Division: `=[Column1] / [Column2]`

Using Functions

Microsoft Lists supports a variety of functions, grouped into categories such as mathematical, text, date and time, logical, and lookup functions. Here are some common functions and their usage:

1. Mathematical Functions:

  - `SUM`: Adds up values. Example: `=SUM([Column1], [Column2], [Column3])`

  - `AVERAGE`: Calculates the average of values. Example: `=AVERAGE([Column1], [Column2])`

  - `MIN` and `MAX`: Finds the minimum or maximum value. Example: `=MIN([Column1], [Column2])`, `=MAX([Column1], [Column2])`

2. Text Functions:

  - `CONCATENATE`: Combines multiple text values. Example: `=CONCATENATE([FirstName], " ", [LastName])`

  - `LEFT`, `RIGHT`: Extracts a specified number of characters from a text string. Example: `=LEFT([TextColumn], 5)`, `=RIGHT([TextColumn], 3)`

  - `LEN`: Returns the length of a text string. Example: `=LEN([TextColumn])`

3. Date and Time Functions:

   - `TODAY`: Returns the current date. Example: `=TODAY()`

   - `YEAR`, `MONTH`, `DAY`: Extracts the year, month, or day from a date. Example: `=YEAR([DateColumn])`, `=MONTH([DateColumn])`, `=DAY([DateColumn])`

   - `DATEDIF`: Calculates the difference between two dates. Example: `=DATEDIF([StartDate], [EndDate], "d")` (where "d" denotes days)

4. Logical Functions:

   - `IF`: Performs a logical test and returns different values based on the result. Example: `=IF([Column1] > 10, "Yes", "No")`

   - `AND`, `OR`: Combines multiple logical conditions. Example: `=AND([Column1] > 10, [Column2] < 20)`, `=OR([Column1] > 10, [Column2] < 20)`

Practical Examples

To better understand the application of calculated columns, let's explore some practical examples.

1. Calculating Total Cost:

   Suppose you have a list for tracking orders, with columns for `Quantity` and `Unit Price`. You can create a calculated column to compute the total cost for each order using the formula:

   =[Quantity] [Unit Price]

2. Combining Text Columns:

   If you have separate columns for `First Name` and `Last Name`, and you want to create a full name column, use the following formula:

   =[First Name] & " " & [Last Name]

3. Age Calculation:

For a list with a `Date of Birth` column, you can calculate the age of individuals using:

=YEAR(TODAY()) - YEAR([Date of Birth])

4. Status Based on Date:

Assume you have a `Due Date` column and want to mark items as "Overdue" or "On Time". Use the following formula:

=IF([Due Date] < TODAY(), "Overdue", "On Time")

Best Practices for Using Calculated Columns

1. Keep It Simple: Start with simple formulas and gradually add complexity. This approach makes it easier to troubleshoot errors.

2. Consistent Naming: Use clear and consistent names for your columns to make formulas easier to read and understand.

3. Testing: Test your formulas with different data to ensure they work as expected in all scenarios.

4. Documentation: Document your formulas and the logic behind them, especially for complex calculations. This practice is helpful for future reference and for others who may work with your lists.

5. Performance Considerations: Be mindful of performance impacts when using complex formulas on large datasets. Test and optimize your formulas as needed.

Troubleshooting Formula Errors

1. Syntax Errors: Ensure your formula syntax is correct. Check for missing or extra parentheses, commas, and other symbols.

2. Invalid Column References: Verify that the column names used in your formulas match the actual column names in the list.

3. Data Type Mismatch: Ensure the data types of columns used in calculations are compatible. For example, you cannot perform arithmetic operations on text columns.

4. Function Limitations: Be aware of the limitations of the functions you are using. Not all Excel functions are available in Microsoft Lists.

Conclusion

Calculated columns in Microsoft Lists are a powerful feature that can significantly enhance your data management capabilities. By leveraging formulas and functions, you can automate calculations, improve data accuracy, and generate valuable insights directly within your lists. Whether you are performing simple arithmetic operations or creating complex logical expressions, understanding how to effectively use calculated columns will help you get the most out of Microsoft Lists. As you become more comfortable with creating and applying formulas, you'll be able to tackle more advanced scenarios and further streamline your workflows.

This section provided an in-depth look at creating formulas in calculated columns, covering the basics, exploring various functions, and presenting practical examples. In the next section, we will continue our exploration of calculated columns by examining more advanced use cases and practical examples to further demonstrate their utility in managing data within Microsoft Lists.

Practical Examples of Calculated Columns

Calculated columns in Microsoft Lists provide a powerful way to automate data processing and enhance the functionality of your lists. By using calculated columns, you can create dynamic and context-sensitive data that updates automatically based on other list fields. This section will delve into practical examples of calculated columns, illustrating their versatility and how they can be leveraged to solve real-world problems.

Example 1: Calculating Total Cost

One common use of calculated columns is to compute totals based on other fields in the list. For instance, imagine you have a list that tracks inventory items, and you want to calculate the total cost of each item based on the unit price and the quantity.

1. Create the Columns:

  - Unit Price (Number)

  - Quantity (Number)

  - Total Cost (Calculated)

2. Define the Formula:

  - In the "Total Cost" calculated column, use the formula: `=[Unit Price][Quantity]`.

This simple calculation ensures that the total cost is automatically updated whenever the unit price or quantity changes, providing an accurate and real-time total cost for each inventory item.

Example 2: Calculating Age from Birthdate

Another useful application of calculated columns is calculating the age of individuals based on their birthdate. This is particularly useful for HR lists or membership databases.

1. Create the Columns:

  - Birthdate (Date and Time)

  - Age (Calculated)

2. Define the Formula:

  - In the "Age" calculated column, use the formula: `=DATEDIF([Birthdate], TODAY(), "Y")`.

This formula calculates the difference between the current date and the birthdate, outputting the age in years. The DATEDIF function is particularly useful for date calculations, allowing you to measure the difference in various units such as days, months, or years.

Example 3: Flagging Overdue Tasks

For project management lists, it's often important to identify tasks that are overdue. A calculated column can be used to flag these tasks automatically.

1. Create the Columns:

  - Due Date (Date and Time)

  - Status (Choice: "Not Started", "In Progress", "Completed")

  - Overdue (Calculated)

2. Define the Formula:

  - In the "Overdue" calculated column, use the formula: `=IF(AND([Status] <> "Completed", [Due Date] < TODAY()), "Yes", "No")`.

This formula checks if the task is not completed and if the due date is earlier than today's date. If both conditions are true, the "Overdue" column will display "Yes"; otherwise, it will display "No". This helps in quickly identifying tasks that need immediate attention.

Example 4: Concatenating Text Fields

Concatenating text fields is another practical use of calculated columns, especially when you need to combine information from multiple fields into one.

1. Create the Columns:

  - First Name (Single line of text)

  - Last Name (Single line of text)

  - Full Name (Calculated)

2. Define the Formula:

  - In the "Full Name" calculated column, use the formula: `=[First Name] & " " & [Last Name]`.

This formula combines the first and last names into a single full name field, separated by a space. This is useful for lists where you want to display the full name of individuals without having to enter it manually.

Example 5: Calculating Progress Percentage

For task management or project tracking, calculating the progress percentage based on completed tasks can provide valuable insights into overall project status.

1. Create the Columns:

  - Total Tasks (Number)

  - Completed Tasks (Number)

  - Progress (Calculated)

2. Define the Formula:

  - In the "Progress" calculated column, use the formula: `=([Completed Tasks]/[Total Tasks])100`.

This formula calculates the percentage of completed tasks relative to the total number of tasks. It provides a clear visual indicator of progress, which can be particularly useful in project dashboards or reports.

Example 6: Determining Task Priority

You can use calculated columns to set task priorities based on due dates and current status, helping to prioritize tasks effectively.

1. Create the Columns:

  - Due Date (Date and Time)

  - Status (Choice: "Not Started", "In Progress", "Completed")

  - Priority (Calculated)

2. Define the Formula:

  - In the "Priority" calculated column, use the formula: `=IF([Status] = "Completed", "Low", IF([Due Date] < TODAY() + 7, "High", "Medium"))`.

This formula assigns a "High" priority to tasks due within the next week, a "Medium" priority to other pending tasks, and a "Low" priority to completed tasks. This helps in focusing on tasks that are approaching their deadlines.

Example 7: Calculating Discounts

For sales or invoice lists, you can calculate discounts based on predefined criteria such as quantity purchased.

1. Create the Columns:

 - Quantity (Number)

 - Unit Price (Number)

 - Discount (Calculated)

2. Define the Formula:

 - In the "Discount" calculated column, use the formula: `=IF([Quantity] >= 100, [Unit Price]0.1, IF([Quantity] >= 50, [Unit Price]0.05, 0))`.

This formula applies a 10% discount for quantities of 100 or more, a 5% discount for quantities between 50 and 99, and no discount for quantities below 50. This automated discount calculation ensures accuracy and saves time.

Example 8: Generating Unique Identifiers

In some cases, you might need to generate unique identifiers for list items. A calculated column can concatenate fields to create a unique ID.

1. Create the Columns:

 - ID (Number)

 - Category (Choice)

 - Unique ID (Calculated)

2. Define the Formula:

 - In the "Unique ID" calculated column, use the formula: `=[Category] & "-" & TEXT([ID],"000")`.

This formula combines the category with a zero-padded ID number to create a unique identifier like "HR-001" or "IT-045". This approach is particularly useful for lists that require unique codes for each entry.

Example 9: Calculating Work Hours

For time tracking lists, calculating the total work hours between start and end times can be automated using calculated columns.

1. Create the Columns:

  - Start Time (Date and Time)

  - End Time (Date and Time)

  - Total Hours (Calculated)

2. Define the Formula:

  - In the "Total Hours" calculated column, use the formula: `=([End Time] - [Start Time])24`.

This formula calculates the difference in hours between the start and end times. Multiplying by 24 converts the result from days to hours. This is useful for tracking the duration of tasks or shifts.

Example 10: Dynamic Status Updates

You can use calculated columns to automatically update the status of list items based on various criteria, such as due dates or progress percentages.

1. Create the Columns:

  - Due Date (Date and Time)

  - Progress (Number)

  - Status (Calculated)

2. Define the Formula:

- In the "Status" calculated column, use the formula: `=IF([Progress] = 100, "Completed", IF([Due Date] < TODAY(), "Overdue", "In Progress"))`.

This formula sets the status to "Completed" if progress is 100%, "Overdue" if the due date has passed, and "In Progress" otherwise. This dynamic update helps in keeping track of the current status without manual intervention.

Example 11: Employee Tenure Calculation

For HR lists, calculating employee tenure based on their hire date can be useful for various analyses and reports.

1. Create the Columns:

  - Hire Date (Date and Time)

  - Tenure (Calculated)

2. Define the Formula:

  - In the "Tenure" calculated column, use the formula: `=DATEDIF([Hire Date], TODAY(), "Y")`.

This formula calculates the number of years an employee has been with the company, providing a quick overview of employee tenure.

Example 12: Monthly Expense Summarization

For financial tracking lists, summarizing monthly expenses can be automated using calculated columns.

1. Create the Columns:

  - Expense Date (Date and Time)

  - Amount (Currency)

  - Month-Year (Calculated)

2. Define the Formula:

- In the "Month-Year" calculated column, use the formula: `=TEXT([Expense Date], "MMM-YYYY")`.

This formula extracts the month and year from the expense date, allowing you to group and summarize expenses by month and year.

Conclusion

Calculated columns in Microsoft Lists offer immense flexibility and power, enabling users to automate complex data processing tasks and enhance the functionality of their lists. By leveraging these practical examples, you can significantly improve the efficiency and accuracy of your data management processes. Whether you're calculating totals, determining priorities, or generating unique identifiers, calculated columns provide the tools you need to streamline your workflows and achieve better organization with Microsoft Lists.

CHAPTER VI
Visualizing Data with Microsoft Lists

6.1 Creating Charts and Graphs

Using Built-in Visualization Tools

Visualizing data is a crucial aspect of data management and analysis. Microsoft Lists offers built-in visualization tools that allow users to create charts and graphs to represent their data more effectively. These visualizations help in identifying trends, patterns, and anomalies, making it easier to derive insights and make informed decisions. In this section, we will explore how to use these built-in tools to create various types of visual representations of your data.

Understanding the Importance of Data Visualization

Before diving into the specifics of using built-in visualization tools in Microsoft Lists, it's essential to understand why data visualization is important. Data visualization transforms complex data sets into graphical representations, making it easier to understand and interpret. It allows users to see relationships between data points, identify trends, and detect outliers. Effective data visualization can lead to better decision-making, improved communication, and enhanced data storytelling.

Getting Started with Built-in Visualization Tools

Microsoft Lists provides several options for visualizing data directly within the platform. These tools are user-friendly and do not require advanced technical skills, making them accessible to a wide range of users. To begin using these tools, follow these steps:

1. Open Your List: Start by opening the list you want to visualize. Ensure that your data is well-organized and complete, as this will impact the quality of your visualizations.

2. Access Visualization Options: In the command bar at the top of the list, you will find various options for creating visualizations. Look for options like "Visualize" or "Charts" depending on the specific implementation and updates of Microsoft Lists.

3. Choose a Visualization Type: Microsoft Lists offers different types of charts and graphs, including bar charts, line charts, pie charts, and more. Select the type of visualization that best suits your data and the insights you want to derive.

Creating Different Types of Charts and Graphs

1. Bar Charts:

   - When to Use: Bar charts are ideal for comparing different categories or groups. They are useful for visualizing data that is divided into distinct categories.

   - How to Create: Select "Bar Chart" from the visualization options. Choose the data columns that represent the categories and values you want to compare. Customize the appearance and settings as needed.

2. Line Charts:

   - When to Use: Line charts are perfect for showing trends over time. They are commonly used for time series data where the x-axis represents time intervals.

   - How to Create: Select "Line Chart" from the visualization options. Choose the columns that represent the time intervals and the corresponding data values. Customize the chart to highlight key trends and patterns.

3. Pie Charts:

   - When to Use: Pie charts are best for showing proportions and percentages. They provide a visual representation of how different parts contribute to a whole.

- How to Create: Select "Pie Chart" from the visualization options. Choose the column that represents the categories and the column that represents the values. Adjust the chart settings to display percentages and labels.

4. Column Charts:

- When to Use: Column charts are similar to bar charts but are displayed vertically. They are suitable for comparing data across different categories.

- How to Create: Select "Column Chart" from the visualization options. Choose the columns for categories and values, and customize the chart's appearance.

Customizing Your Visualizations

After selecting the type of chart or graph and the corresponding data, you can further customize your visualizations to enhance clarity and effectiveness. Here are some customization options available in Microsoft Lists:

1. Labels and Titles: Add meaningful labels and titles to your charts and graphs to provide context. This includes chart titles, axis labels, and data labels.

2. Colors and Themes: Customize the colors and themes of your visualizations to match your branding or preferences. Consistent use of colors can help differentiate between different data points.

3. Legends and Data Points: Enable legends to explain what different colors or symbols represent. Show or hide data points to focus on specific parts of the data.

4. Gridlines and Axes: Adjust the gridlines and axes settings to improve readability. You can choose to display or hide gridlines and customize the scale of the axes.

Practical Examples

1. Sales Performance Analysis:

- Scenario: You have a list of monthly sales data for different products and regions. You want to visualize the sales performance over the past year.

- Solution: Create a line chart with months on the x-axis and sales figures on the y-axis. Use different lines to represent different products or regions. Customize the chart to highlight key trends and seasonal patterns.

2. Project Task Status:

   - Scenario: You manage a project with multiple tasks, and you want to visualize the status of each task.

   - Solution: Create a column chart with task names on the x-axis and task completion percentage on the y-axis. Use different colors to represent different status categories (e.g., not started, in progress, completed). Customize the chart to display the overall project progress.

3. Budget Allocation:

   - Scenario: You have a list of budget allocations for different departments and want to visualize how the budget is distributed.

   - Solution: Create a pie chart with department names as categories and budget amounts as values. Customize the chart to display percentages and add a legend to explain the colors.

Benefits of Using Built-in Visualization Tools

Using built-in visualization tools in Microsoft Lists offers several benefits:

1. Ease of Use: These tools are designed to be user-friendly, allowing users to create visualizations without extensive technical knowledge.

2. Integration: Visualizations created within Microsoft Lists can be easily integrated with other Microsoft 365 apps, such as Teams and SharePoint, enhancing collaboration and data sharing.

3. Real-time Updates: Visualizations are linked to the underlying data in the list, ensuring that any updates to the data are automatically reflected in the charts and graphs.

4. Improved Decision-making: Visual representations of data help in quickly identifying trends, patterns, and outliers, leading to better and faster decision-making.

Best Practices for Creating Effective Visualizations

1. Keep It Simple: Avoid cluttering your visualizations with too much information. Focus on the key data points and insights you want to convey.

2. Use Consistent Colors and Styles: Consistency in colors and styles helps in making your visualizations more readable and professional-looking.

3. Provide Context: Always provide context through titles, labels, and legends. This ensures that the audience understands what the visualization represents.

4. Highlight Important Data: Use formatting options to highlight important data points or trends. This draws attention to critical information.

Conclusion

Microsoft Lists' built-in visualization tools are powerful features that enable users to transform raw data into meaningful insights. By understanding how to create and customize charts and graphs, users can effectively communicate their data and make informed decisions. Whether you are tracking sales performance, managing project tasks, or analyzing budget allocations, these visualization tools will help you unlock the full potential of your data.

In the next section, we will explore how to enhance your visualizations further by integrating Microsoft Lists with Power BI, a more advanced data visualization tool that offers additional capabilities and flexibility.

Integrating with Power BI

Integrating Microsoft Lists with Power BI brings powerful data visualization and business intelligence capabilities to your fingertips. Power BI allows you to transform raw data from your lists into meaningful insights through interactive dashboards and reports. This section will guide you through the process of connecting Microsoft Lists to Power BI, creating visualizations, and leveraging the integration to enhance your data analysis.

Understanding Power BI

Power BI is a suite of business analytics tools by Microsoft designed to analyze data and share insights. With Power BI, you can:

- Connect to various data sources

- Transform and clean data

- Create interactive visualizations and reports

- Share and collaborate on reports with others

Benefits of Integrating Microsoft Lists with Power BI

Integrating Microsoft Lists with Power BI offers numerous benefits:

1. Enhanced Data Visualization: Create sophisticated charts and graphs that are more visually appealing and informative than the built-in options in Microsoft Lists.

2. Interactive Dashboards: Build interactive dashboards that allow you to drill down into data and uncover insights.

3. Advanced Analytics: Utilize Power BI's advanced analytics features, such as AI-driven insights and custom calculations, to analyze your list data.

4. Seamless Data Refresh: Set up automatic data refreshes to ensure your visualizations are always up to date.

5. Collaboration and Sharing: Share your Power BI reports and dashboards with colleagues, allowing for collaborative analysis and decision-making.

Connecting Microsoft Lists to Power BI

To start integrating Microsoft Lists with Power BI, follow these steps:

1. Prepare Your Data in Microsoft Lists

   - Ensure your list data is clean and well-structured. Power BI works best with organized data, so take the time to remove any inconsistencies or duplicates.

2. Open Power BI Desktop

- Download and install Power BI Desktop from the Microsoft website if you haven't already.

- Open Power BI Desktop and start a new project.

3. Connect to Microsoft Lists

 - In Power BI Desktop, click on "Get Data" from the Home ribbon.

 - Select "More" to open the Get Data window.

 - In the Get Data window, search for "SharePoint Online List" and select it. Click "Connect."

 - Enter the URL of your SharePoint site where your Microsoft List is located. Click "OK."

 - Power BI will display a list of available lists. Select the list you want to visualize and click "Load."

4. Transform and Clean Data (Optional)

 - Power BI's Query Editor will open, allowing you to transform and clean your data. You can remove unnecessary columns, filter rows, and apply transformations to prepare your data for analysis.

 - Once your data is ready, click "Close & Apply" to load it into Power BI.

Creating Visualizations in Power BI

With your Microsoft Lists data loaded into Power BI, you can start creating visualizations:

1. Build a Basic Chart

 - In the Visualizations pane, select the type of chart you want to create (e.g., bar chart, line chart, pie chart).

 - Drag and drop fields from your list data into the Values, Axis, and Legend areas of the chart.

 - Customize the chart by adjusting settings in the Format pane.

2. Create Interactive Dashboards

 - Add multiple visualizations to a single report page to create a dashboard.

- Use slicers and filters to make your dashboard interactive, allowing users to explore different aspects of the data.

- Link visualizations so that selecting a data point in one chart highlights related data in other charts.

3. Leverage Advanced Features

- Utilize Power BI's advanced features, such as DAX (Data Analysis Expressions) for custom calculations, to enhance your visualizations.

- Explore AI-driven insights by enabling the "Analyze" feature on your visualizations to discover patterns and trends.

Publishing and Sharing Your Reports

Once you have created your visualizations and dashboards, you can publish and share them with others:

1. Publish to Power BI Service

- Click on the "Publish" button in Power BI Desktop.

- Sign in to your Power BI account and select the workspace where you want to publish your report.

- After publishing, your report will be available in the Power BI Service.

2. Share with Colleagues

- In the Power BI Service, navigate to your report and click on the "Share" button.

- Enter the email addresses of the colleagues you want to share the report with and set their access permissions.

- You can also generate a shareable link to your report.

3. Embed in SharePoint or Teams

- Embed your Power BI report in a SharePoint page or a Microsoft Teams channel for easy access and collaboration.

- In SharePoint, add a Power BI web part to your page and select your report.

- In Teams, use the Power BI app to add your report as a tab in a channel.

Best Practices for Integrating Microsoft Lists with Power BI

To make the most of the integration between Microsoft Lists and Power BI, consider these best practices:

1. Organize Your Data

- Keep your Microsoft Lists data organized and clean. Regularly update and maintain your lists to ensure data quality.

2. Plan Your Visualizations

- Before creating visualizations, plan what insights you want to derive from your data. Think about the questions you want to answer and design your charts accordingly.

3. Use Consistent Formatting

- Apply consistent formatting across your visualizations to create a cohesive and professional look. Use the same color schemes, fonts, and chart styles.

4. Optimize for Performance

- Large datasets can slow down Power BI performance. Optimize your data by filtering out unnecessary records and aggregating data where possible.

5. Test and Iterate

- Test your visualizations with end-users and gather feedback. Iterate on your designs to improve usability and effectiveness.

Real-World Use Cases

Integrating Microsoft Lists with Power BI can be applied in various real-world scenarios:

1. Project Management

- Track project progress and visualize timelines, task completion rates, and resource allocation using Gantt charts and other visualizations.

2. Sales and Marketing

- Analyze sales data, track leads and opportunities, and measure campaign performance with dynamic dashboards and interactive charts.

3. Human Resources

- Monitor employee data, track recruitment metrics, and analyze workforce trends with comprehensive reports and visualizations.

4. Operations and Logistics

- Visualize supply chain data, track inventory levels, and optimize logistics operations with insightful charts and dashboards.

Conclusion

Integrating Microsoft Lists with Power BI unlocks a powerful combination of data management and visualization capabilities. By following the steps outlined in this section, you can transform your list data into interactive, informative visualizations that drive better decision-making and business outcomes. Whether you are a project manager, sales analyst, HR professional, or operations manager, the integration of Microsoft Lists with Power BI can help you gain deeper insights and achieve greater efficiency in your work.

By mastering the integration between Microsoft Lists and Power BI, you can harness the full potential of your data, turning raw information into actionable insights that propel your organization forward.

6.2 Conditional Formatting

Conditional formatting in Microsoft Lists allows you to apply specific formatting to list items based on predefined criteria. This powerful feature helps you highlight important data, identify trends, and improve data readability. In this section, we will delve into setting up conditional formatting rules to make your lists more visually informative and easier to analyze.

Setting Up Conditional Formatting Rules

1. Introduction to Conditional Formatting

Conditional formatting is a feature that dynamically changes the appearance of list items based on the conditions you specify. These conditions can be based on the values in your list columns, allowing you to create visual cues that draw attention to specific items or ranges of data. For instance, you can highlight overdue tasks, flag high-priority items, or differentiate between different categories of data.

2. Accessing Conditional Formatting

To set up conditional formatting in Microsoft Lists, follow these steps:

1. Open the Microsoft Lists app and navigate to the list where you want to apply conditional formatting.

2. Click on the column header for the column you want to format.

3. From the dropdown menu, select "Column settings" and then "Format this column."

4. In the column formatting pane, click on "Add formatting" under the Conditional formatting section.

3. Understanding Conditional Formatting Options

When setting up conditional formatting, you have several options to choose from:

- Format by Rules: This option allows you to define rules based on the values in your list columns. You can specify different formatting styles for different conditions.

- Format by Range: Use this option to apply formatting based on a range of values. For example, you can use a color gradient to show the progression of data values.

- Advanced Mode: For more complex scenarios, the advanced mode provides a JSON editor where you can define intricate formatting rules using JSON syntax.

4. Creating Basic Conditional Formatting Rules

Let's start with a basic example. Suppose you have a task list and you want to highlight overdue tasks in red. Follow these steps:

1. Choose the Column: Select the column that contains the due dates.

2. Add a Rule: In the formatting pane, click on "Add a rule."

3. Define the Condition: Set the condition to highlight items where the due date is before today's date. Use the condition "is before" and enter `=today()`.

4. Set the Formatting Style: Choose a formatting style, such as changing the text color to red or setting a red background.

5. Save the Rule: Click on "Save" to apply the rule.

Now, all overdue tasks will be highlighted in red, making them easily identifiable.

5. Applying Multiple Rules

You can apply multiple conditional formatting rules to a single column. For example, in your task list, you might want to highlight high-priority tasks in yellow and overdue tasks in red. To do this:

1. Add a Rule for High-Priority Tasks: Follow the steps above to add a new rule. Set the condition to "Priority equals High" and choose a yellow formatting style.

2. Add a Rule for Overdue Tasks: Add another rule with the condition "Due Date is before today" and choose a red formatting style.

3. Save All Rules: Make sure all rules are saved. The list will now show high-priority tasks in yellow and overdue tasks in red.

6. Using Conditional Formatting with Different Data Types

Conditional formatting is versatile and can be applied to various data types, including text, numbers, dates, and choice fields. Here are some examples:

- Text Fields: Highlight items based on specific keywords. For instance, mark items containing "urgent" in bold.

- Number Fields: Use color scales to show ranges. For example, apply a green-to-red gradient to a sales column to indicate performance.

- Date Fields: Highlight upcoming events. For example, use green for events happening this week and yellow for next week.

- Choice Fields: Apply different colors to different categories. For instance, in a status field, mark "Completed" in green, "In Progress" in blue, and "Pending" in orange.

7. Customizing Conditional Formatting with JSON

For advanced users, customizing conditional formatting with JSON provides greater flexibility. JSON (JavaScript Object Notation) allows you to define complex rules and apply intricate formatting styles. Here's a basic example of a JSON rule that changes the background color based on priority levels

In this example, the background color changes to red for high priority, yellow for medium priority, and green for low priority. To apply this JSON rule:

1. Open Column Formatting Pane: Click on the column header, select "Column settings," and then "Format this column."

2. Switch to Advanced Mode: In the formatting pane, click on "Advanced mode."

3. Paste the JSON Code: Copy and paste the JSON code into the editor.

4. Save the Changes: Click "Save" to apply the formatting.

8. Best Practices for Conditional Formatting

To make the most of conditional formatting, consider the following best practices:

- Keep It Simple: Avoid overloading your lists with too many rules, as this can make the data harder to read.

- Use Meaningful Colors: Choose colors that convey the right message. For example, use red for critical issues and green for completed tasks.

- Test Your Rules: Before applying to production lists, test your conditional formatting rules on a sample list to ensure they work as expected.

- Document Your Rules: Maintain documentation of the rules you apply, especially in collaborative environments, so that others understand the logic behind the formatting.

9. Troubleshooting Conditional Formatting

If your conditional formatting rules are not working as expected:

- Check Conditions: Ensure that the conditions are correctly defined and the syntax is correct.

- Review Data Types: Make sure the data types in your list columns match the conditions you've set.

- Clear Conflicts: If multiple rules apply to the same column, check for conflicts and adjust the order of the rules if necessary.

- Validate JSON: If using JSON, validate the code for syntax errors using online JSON validators.

10. Conclusion

Setting up conditional formatting rules in Microsoft Lists enhances the visual representation of your data, making it easier to analyze and act upon. By understanding and applying these rules effectively, you can transform raw data into meaningful insights, improve productivity, and ensure critical information stands out.

By following the steps outlined in this section, you will be well-equipped to create and manage conditional formatting rules that meet your specific needs, thereby maximizing the utility of Microsoft Lists in your organizational workflows.

Practical Applications of Conditional Formatting

Conditional formatting in Microsoft Lists is a powerful tool that enables users to highlight data based on specific criteria, making it easier to analyze and understand information quickly. By applying different formatting rules, you can visually differentiate data points, identify trends, and draw attention to critical items. Here, we'll explore several practical applications of conditional formatting to help you maximize its potential in your lists.

1. Highlighting Overdue Tasks

One of the most common uses of conditional formatting is to highlight overdue tasks in a task management list. This can help ensure that team members are aware of deadlines that have been missed and can take prompt action to address them.

Steps to highlight overdue tasks:

- Go to the list where your tasks are stored.

- Open the column settings for the due date column.

- Create a new formatting rule.

- Set the rule to check if the due date is less than today's date.

- Choose a formatting style, such as changing the background color to red or making the text bold.

Example:

If your task list includes a "Due Date" column, you can set a rule that highlights any tasks with a due date that is earlier than today. This visual cue makes it easy to spot overdue tasks at a glance.

2. Flagging High-Priority Items

Another useful application is flagging high-priority items. In a project management list, you might have tasks with different priority levels. Using conditional formatting, you can highlight high-priority tasks to ensure they receive the attention they deserve.

Steps to flag high-priority items:

- Identify the column that contains the priority level, such as "Priority."

- Create a new formatting rule for this column.

- Set the rule to apply formatting when the priority level is "High."

- Choose a distinct formatting style, such as a bright background color or a bold font.

Example:

In a "Priority" column, you can create a rule that highlights all tasks labeled as "High Priority" with a bright yellow background. This ensures that these tasks stand out, making it easier for team members to focus on them.

3. Visualizing Status Updates

Conditional formatting can also be used to visualize status updates in a list. For instance, in a bug tracking list, you can use different colors to represent various bug statuses such as "Open," "In Progress," "Resolved," and "Closed."

Steps to visualize status updates:

- Locate the column that contains the status information, such as "Status."

- Create multiple formatting rules, one for each status type.

- Assign a unique color to each status to distinguish them visually.

Example:

You can set up rules so that bugs marked as "Open" are highlighted in red, "In Progress" in orange, "Resolved" in green, and "Closed" in gray. This color-coding helps team members quickly understand the current state of bugs without reading the text.

4. Identifying Top Performers

In performance tracking lists, conditional formatting can be used to identify top performers based on specific metrics. This is particularly useful in sales or academic environments where recognizing high achievers is essential.

Steps to identify top performers:

- Choose the column that contains the performance metric, such as "Sales" or "Score."

- Create a new formatting rule to highlight values above a certain threshold.

- Apply a distinct formatting style to these top performers.

Example:

If you have a "Sales" column, you can create a rule that highlights any sales figures above a certain amount with a gold background. This visual distinction makes it easy to spot top-performing sales representatives.

5. Monitoring Inventory Levels

In inventory management lists, conditional formatting can help monitor stock levels and flag items that need restocking. This ensures that you can maintain optimal inventory levels and avoid stockouts.

Steps to monitor inventory levels:

- Identify the column that contains inventory levels, such as "Quantity."

- Create a formatting rule to highlight items with low stock levels.

- Choose a formatting style, such as a red background for low stock items.

Example:

In a "Quantity" column, you can set a rule that highlights any item with a quantity below a predefined threshold (e.g., less than 10 units) in red. This alert helps inventory managers to quickly identify and reorder low stock items.

6. Emphasizing Critical Data

Conditional formatting can emphasize critical data points in a variety of contexts. For example, in a financial report list, you can highlight expenses that exceed a certain amount to draw attention to significant expenditures.

Steps to emphasize critical data:

- Select the column that contains the critical data, such as "Expense Amount."

- Create a formatting rule to highlight values that exceed a specific threshold.

- Apply a formatting style that makes these values stand out.

Example:

In an "Expense Amount" column, you can create a rule that highlights any expense over $1,000 with a bold font and a blue background. This visual cue ensures that large expenditures are easily noticed and reviewed.

7. Differentiating Data Categories

Conditional formatting can be used to differentiate data categories visually. This is useful in lists where different categories need to be easily distinguishable, such as a list of products grouped by category.

Steps to differentiate data categories:

- Identify the column that contains the category information, such as "Product Category."

- Create a formatting rule for each category.

- Assign a unique color to each category.

Example:

In a "Product Category" column, you can set up rules to highlight electronics in blue, clothing in green, and home goods in yellow. This color-coding helps users quickly identify the category of each product.

8. Tracking Project Milestones

In project management, tracking milestones is crucial for ensuring projects stay on track. Conditional formatting can highlight milestones that are approaching or overdue.

Steps to track project milestones:

- Choose the column that contains milestone dates, such as "Milestone Date."

- Create a formatting rule to highlight milestones approaching within a certain time frame (e.g., within the next week).

- Apply a distinct formatting style for overdue milestones.

Example:

In a "Milestone Date" column, you can create a rule that highlights milestones due within the next 7 days in yellow and overdue milestones in red. This visual cue helps project managers stay aware of upcoming and missed deadlines.

9. Highlighting Data Based on Custom Criteria

Conditional formatting allows you to create custom rules based on unique criteria specific to your needs. This flexibility makes it possible to tailor your lists to highlight the most relevant data points.

Steps to highlight data based on custom criteria:

- Identify the column(s) that contain the data you want to highlight.

- Create custom formatting rules based on your criteria.

- Choose formatting styles that best represent your needs.

Example:

If you have a list tracking customer feedback, you can set up rules to highlight feedback scores above 4 with a green background and scores below 2 with a red background. This helps quickly identify positive and negative feedback.

10. Enhancing Visual Appeal

Beyond functionality, conditional formatting can enhance the visual appeal of your lists, making them more attractive and engaging. This can improve user experience and encourage better interaction with the data.

Steps to enhance visual appeal:

- Choose a column or multiple columns for formatting.

- Create rules that apply complementary colors and styles.

- Ensure the formatting enhances readability without overwhelming the user.

Example:

In a "Status" column, you can create rules that use pastel colors to indicate different statuses. This subtle use of color improves the visual appeal of the list while maintaining clarity.

By leveraging these practical applications of conditional formatting, you can transform your Microsoft Lists into dynamic, visually engaging tools that enhance data analysis, improve workflow efficiency, and support better decision-making. Whether you're managing tasks, tracking performance, or monitoring inventory, conditional formatting offers endless possibilities to customize your lists according to your specific needs.

6.3 Using Calendar and Gallery Views

Creating and Using Calendar Views

Microsoft Lists is a powerful tool for organizing and managing data. One of its standout features is the ability to visualize data in various formats, including calendar views. This capability is particularly useful for tasks that are time-sensitive or schedule-driven, such as project management, event planning, and tracking deadlines.

Creating Calendar Views

Creating a calendar view in Microsoft Lists allows you to see your list items in a date-centric format. Here's a step-by-step guide to creating and using calendar views:

1. Accessing Calendar View Creation

Begin by navigating to the list you want to visualize. Click on the "All Items" dropdown, then select "Create new view."

2. Selecting Calendar View

In the view creation options, choose "Calendar" as the view type. This option sets the foundation for displaying your list items in a calendar format.

3. Configuring Calendar Settings

- View Name: Provide a name for your calendar view that clearly indicates its purpose, such as "Project Deadlines" or "Event Schedule."

- Month View and Week View: Configure the calendar to display by month or week. This setting determines how much information you see at a glance.

- Start and End Dates: Specify the list columns that contain the start and end dates. These dates will be used to plot the items on the calendar.

4. Customizing Calendar Appearance

- Color Coding: Use color-coding to differentiate between types of events or tasks. For instance, project deadlines could be in red, meetings in blue, and milestones in green.

- Additional Fields: Choose additional fields to display on the calendar entries, such as location, assigned person, or priority.

5. Saving and Viewing the Calendar

Once you have configured all settings, save the view. Your list items will now be displayed on the calendar according to the start and end dates you specified.

Using Calendar Views

With the calendar view created, it's essential to know how to use it effectively. Here are some tips and best practices:

1. Navigating the Calendar

- Switching Views: Easily switch between month, week, and day views to get different perspectives on your schedule.

- Scrolling and Zooming: Scroll through months or weeks to navigate through time, and zoom in on specific dates for detailed views.

2. Interacting with Calendar Items

- Creating New Items: Add new items directly from the calendar by clicking on a date. This feature allows for quick entry of tasks or events.

- Editing Items: Click on any calendar entry to edit its details. Changes made here are reflected in the list and vice versa.

- Drag-and-Drop: Some calendar views support drag-and-drop functionality, enabling you to reschedule items quickly by dragging them to new dates.

3. Filtering and Sorting

- Filters: Apply filters to your calendar view to focus on specific items. For instance, filter by project, department, or priority level.

- Sorting: Although calendars are inherently sorted by date, additional sorting criteria can be applied within each date cell, such as by priority or assigned person.

4. Integrating with Other Tools

- Outlook Integration: Sync your calendar view with Microsoft Outlook to consolidate your schedule. This integration ensures that you don't miss important deadlines or events.

- Power Automate: Use Power Automate to trigger workflows based on calendar events. For example, automatically send reminders for upcoming deadlines.

Best Practices for Calendar Views

To maximize the effectiveness of calendar views in Microsoft Lists, consider the following best practices:

1. Consistent Data Entry

Ensure that the date fields in your list items are consistently populated. Missing or incorrect dates can result in incomplete or misleading calendar views.

2. Clear and Descriptive Titles

Use clear and descriptive titles for your list items. This practice makes it easier to identify tasks or events at a glance when viewing the calendar.

3. Regular Updates

Regularly update your list items to keep the calendar current. Outdated information can lead to confusion and missed deadlines.

4. Collaborative Use

Encourage team members to use and update the calendar view. Collaboration ensures that everyone is aware of key dates and deadlines, improving overall project management.

5. Review and Optimize

Periodically review your calendar view settings and optimize them based on feedback and usage patterns. Adjust color codes, filters, and additional fields to enhance clarity and usability.

Practical Applications of Calendar Views

Calendar views in Microsoft Lists have numerous practical applications. Here are a few examples:

1. Project Management

   - Milestone Tracking: Use calendar views to track project milestones. Visualizing milestones on a calendar helps in planning and ensures that key deadlines are met.

   - Task Scheduling: Assign and schedule project tasks directly on the calendar. This visualization aids in balancing workloads and avoiding scheduling conflicts.

2. Event Planning

   - Event Schedules: Plan and manage events by scheduling all related activities on the calendar. This method ensures that every detail is accounted for and helps in coordinating resources.

   - Resource Booking: Track resource availability and bookings on the calendar. This approach prevents double bookings and ensures that resources are allocated efficiently.

3. Personal Productivity

   - Daily Planning: Use calendar views to plan your daily tasks. Visualizing tasks on a calendar helps in prioritizing and managing time effectively.

   - Deadline Management: Track personal deadlines and reminders. A calendar view ensures that important dates are not overlooked.

4. Team Collaboration

   - Team Meetings: Schedule and track team meetings on the calendar. Shared calendar views ensure that all team members are aware of meeting times and agendas.

   - Collaboration Milestones: Track collaborative milestones and deadlines. This practice fosters accountability and keeps the team aligned with project goals.

Conclusion

Creating and using calendar views in Microsoft Lists is a powerful way to visualize and manage time-sensitive data. Whether for project management, event planning, or personal productivity, calendar views provide a clear and organized way to track important dates and deadlines. By following best practices and leveraging the integration capabilities of Microsoft 365, you can enhance your workflow and ensure that nothing slips through the cracks.

Setting Up Gallery Views

Gallery views in Microsoft Lists offer a visually engaging way to display your list items, making it easier to browse through data, especially when visual representation is crucial. This view is particularly beneficial for lists containing images, rich text, or other media types. Setting up gallery views involves a series of steps and configurations that transform your data presentation.

Understanding Gallery Views

Gallery views allow list items to be displayed as cards in a grid format. Each card represents a single list item, and this format is ideal for lists where images or media content are prominent. The visual nature of gallery views makes them perfect for project management dashboards, asset libraries, or any scenario where a visual overview is beneficial.

Steps to Set Up Gallery Views

1. Creating a New Gallery View

1. Access Your List: Open the Microsoft Lists app and navigate to the list for which you want to create a gallery view.

2. View Options: Click on the drop-down menu next to the current view name.

3. Create New View: Select "Create new view" from the list of options.

4. Choose View Type: In the view creation menu, choose "Gallery" as the view type.

5. Name Your View: Provide a name for your new gallery view, making it easily identifiable.

6. Save: Click "Create" or "Save" to finalize the creation of your new gallery view.

 2. Configuring Card Layouts

Once the gallery view is created, you need to configure the layout of the cards to ensure they display the most relevant information effectively.

1. Customize Card Layout: Click on the settings icon (gear icon) on the top right corner of the list view and select "Format current view."

2. Card Designer: This opens the card designer interface, where you can drag and drop fields to arrange them as you want them to appear on each card.

3. Add Fields: Add essential fields such as Title, Description, Image, or any other relevant metadata.

4. Card Size and Layout: Adjust the size of the cards to fit the content properly. This can often be found in the layout or settings menu of the card designer.

5. Preview and Adjust: Use the preview pane to see how the cards will look. Make any necessary adjustments to the layout, such as reordering fields or resizing elements.

 3. Adding Images and Media

Gallery views shine when they include visual elements such as images or media files. Ensuring your list items have these elements is crucial for an effective gallery view.

1. Image Columns: Ensure your list has a column dedicated to images or media. If not, you can add a new column by selecting "Add Column" and choosing "Image" as the column type.

2. Upload Images: Populate this column with images for each list item. This can often be done by directly uploading images or linking to image URLs.

3. Thumbnail Settings: If your images are large, configure the thumbnail settings to ensure they are appropriately resized for the gallery view.

 4. Using Conditional Formatting in Gallery Views

Conditional formatting can be used to highlight or emphasize certain list items based on specific criteria, even within gallery views.

1. Access Conditional Formatting: In the card designer interface, navigate to the conditional formatting section.

2. Create Rules: Define rules based on your list's data. For example, you might highlight cards in red if a task is overdue or green if completed.

3. Apply Formats: Set the formatting options such as background color, border, or text color that will be applied when the conditions are met.

 5. Enhancing User Experience with Custom Actions

Adding custom actions to your gallery view can significantly enhance user experience, allowing for quick interactions directly from the card.

1. Custom Actions Setup: In the card designer, look for the custom actions section.

2. Add Actions: Define actions such as "Edit," "Delete," or custom flows that users can trigger directly from the card.

3. Configure: Configure these actions to ensure they are easily accessible and provide the necessary functionality without cluttering the card's interface.

 6. Advanced Customization with JSON

For more advanced users, further customization of gallery views can be achieved through JSON formatting. This allows for greater control over the presentation and interaction elements.

1. Open JSON Editor: In the format view settings, access the JSON editor.

2. Write Custom JSON: Write or paste JSON code to define advanced customizations. This could include conditional visibility, advanced styling, or custom data binding.

3. Preview and Apply: Preview the changes to ensure they work as intended and apply them to see the results in your gallery view.

 7. Testing and Iteration

After setting up the gallery view, it's important to test and iterate to ensure it meets your needs.

1. User Feedback: Share the view with colleagues or team members and gather feedback on usability and effectiveness.

2. Adjust Based on Feedback: Make necessary adjustments based on the feedback received.

3. Monitor Performance: Ensure that the gallery view performs well, especially if it includes high-resolution images or a large number of items.

Best Practices for Gallery Views

- Keep It Simple: Avoid cluttering the card with too much information. Focus on key data points that users need to see at a glance.

- Use High-Quality Images: Ensure images are clear and high-quality to make the gallery view visually appealing.

- Consistent Formatting: Maintain consistent formatting for all cards to provide a uniform look and feel.

- Accessibility: Ensure that the gallery view is accessible to all users, including those using assistive technologies.

Use Cases for Gallery Views

- Project Portfolios: Display project summaries with key details and images.

- Product Catalogs: Show product images, descriptions, and prices in an easily navigable format.

- Event Planning: Visualize event schedules and details with images and important information.

- Employee Directories: Create a visual directory with employee photos and contact information.

Conclusion

Setting up gallery views in Microsoft Lists can transform how you and your team interact with data. By following the steps outlined above, you can create visually appealing, highly functional gallery views that enhance data presentation and user experience. Remember to leverage customization options, such as conditional formatting and custom actions, to make your gallery views even more powerful and tailored to your specific needs.

By mastering gallery views, you'll be able to present your data in an engaging and accessible manner, making it easier for users to navigate, understand, and utilize the information contained within your lists.

CHAPTER VII
Best Practices for Microsoft Lists

7.1 Organizing Lists Effectively

Effective organization is crucial when working with Microsoft Lists, as it ensures that data is easily accessible, understandable, and manageable. One of the foundational aspects of organizing lists effectively is the use of naming conventions and descriptions. These elements provide clarity and context, making it easier for users to understand the purpose and content of each list.

Naming Conventions and Descriptions

1. Importance of Naming Conventions

Naming conventions are standardized guidelines for naming lists, columns, and items within Microsoft Lists. Adopting a consistent naming strategy offers several key benefits:

- Clarity: Clear and descriptive names help users quickly understand the purpose of a list or column.

- Consistency: Uniform naming conventions create a predictable environment, making it easier for users to navigate and locate information.

- Searchability: Well-named lists and columns enhance search functionality, allowing users to find relevant information quickly.

- Scalability: As the number of lists and columns grows, a structured naming convention helps maintain order and prevent confusion.

2. Best Practices for Naming Conventions

To maximize the effectiveness of naming conventions, consider the following best practices:

a. Use Descriptive Names

Descriptive names convey the content and purpose of a list or column. Avoid vague or generic terms that do not provide clear context. For example, instead of naming a list "Project," consider "Project Tasks" or "Project Deadlines."

b. Keep Names Concise

While names should be descriptive, they should also be concise. Long names can be cumbersome and may be truncated in some views. Aim for a balance between clarity and brevity.

c. Incorporate Dates and Versions

For lists and columns that are updated regularly, including dates or version numbers in the name can be helpful. For example, "Sales Report Q1 2024" or "Employee Directory v2."

d. Avoid Special Characters

Special characters can cause issues with sorting and searching. Stick to alphanumeric characters, spaces, and hyphens. For example, use "Monthly-Report" instead of "Monthly_Report!."

e. Use Consistent Formatting

Choose a formatting style and apply it consistently across all lists and columns. For instance, decide whether to use title case ("Project Tasks") or sentence case ("Project tasks") and apply it uniformly.

f. Prefixes and Suffixes

Prefixes and suffixes can be useful for categorizing and grouping related lists. For example, prefixing project-related lists with "Proj-" (e.g., "Proj-Budget," "Proj-Timeline") can help users identify them quickly.

3. Creating Effective Descriptions

Descriptions provide additional context about the purpose and content of a list or column. They are especially useful for new users or when sharing lists with others.

a. Overview of Content

A good description should offer an overview of what the list or column contains. For example, "This list tracks the status and deadlines of all ongoing projects."

b. Purpose and Usage

Include information about the purpose of the list and how it should be used. For example, "Use this list to record and monitor project tasks and their completion status."

c. Instructions and Guidelines

If there are specific guidelines or instructions for using the list, include them in the description. For example, "Please update the task status and completion date as soon as a task is completed."

d. Contact Information

For collaborative lists, providing contact information for the list owner or administrator can be helpful. For example, "For questions or issues, contact John Doe at john.doe@example.com."

4. Examples of Naming Conventions and Descriptions

Here are some examples of well-structured naming conventions and descriptions:

Example 1: Task Management List

- Name: "Team Task Management"

- Description: "This list is used to track tasks assigned to team members, including deadlines, status updates, and priority levels. Please update your task status regularly. For assistance, contact Jane Smith at jane.smith@example.com."

Example 2: Sales Data List

- Name: "Sales Data Q1 2024"

- Description: "This list contains sales data for the first quarter of 2024, including individual sales figures, regional performance, and product category breakdowns. Use this data for quarterly sales analysis and reporting."

Example 3: Project Milestones List

- Name: "Project Milestones - Website Redesign"

- Description: "This list tracks key milestones for the website redesign project. Milestones include design approval, content upload, and final launch. Update milestone status as each stage is completed. Contact Mark Lee at mark.lee@example.com for more information."

5. Implementing Naming Conventions and Descriptions

To implement effective naming conventions and descriptions in Microsoft Lists, follow these steps:

a. Develop a Naming Convention Policy

Create a document outlining your organization's naming convention policy. Include examples and guidelines for naming lists, columns, and items. Ensure that all team members are aware of and follow this policy.

b. Train Users

Provide training sessions or documentation to help users understand the importance of naming conventions and descriptions. Show them how to create effective names and descriptions that adhere to the policy.

c. Monitor and Enforce Compliance

Regularly review lists and columns to ensure compliance with the naming convention policy. Provide feedback and corrections as needed to maintain consistency and clarity.

d. Use Templates

Create list templates with predefined names and descriptions. This can help ensure that new lists are created with consistent naming conventions and descriptions from the start.

e. Review and Update Periodically

As your organization grows and evolves, periodically review and update your naming convention policy to ensure it remains relevant and effective.

Conclusion

Effective organization is a cornerstone of efficient data management in Microsoft Lists. By adopting clear and consistent naming conventions and providing detailed descriptions, you can enhance the usability, searchability, and scalability of your lists. These practices not only improve individual productivity but also contribute to a more organized and collaborative work environment. Implementing these strategies will help ensure that your Microsoft Lists are a powerful tool for managing and organizing information effectively.

Categorizing and Tagging Lists

In the realm of information management, the ability to categorize and tag lists effectively is paramount. Microsoft Lists provides robust features that allow users to organize and classify data with precision. This section explores the importance of categorization and tagging, practical methods for implementation, and best practices to maximize efficiency.

Importance of Categorization and Tagging

Categorization and tagging serve as foundational elements for organizing data within Microsoft Lists. By assigning categories and tags to items, users can quickly locate information based on specific criteria. This systematic approach enhances clarity, accessibility, and usability of lists across various projects and teams.

1. Structuring Categories

Effective categorization begins with defining clear structures that align with organizational goals and operational needs. Establishing a taxonomy tailored to your organization's workflows ensures consistency and ease of navigation within lists. Consider the following strategies:

- Hierarchical Categories: Implement nested categories to reflect hierarchical relationships within your data. This structure aids in drilling down to specific details while maintaining a comprehensive overview.

- Functional Categories: Organize lists based on functional areas or departments within your organization. This approach streamlines access and retrieval of relevant information for respective teams.

2. Implementing Tags

Tags provide flexible metadata that supplement categorization by offering additional descriptors or attributes to list items. Unlike rigid categories, tags offer versatility in labeling items across multiple dimensions. Key considerations include:

- Descriptive Tags: Utilize descriptive keywords or phrases that encapsulate key attributes of list items. This practice enhances searchability and facilitates quick identification of related content.

- Consistent Tagging Practices: Establish guidelines for tagging conventions to ensure uniformity and coherence across lists. Consistent tagging simplifies data retrieval and fosters collaboration by standardizing terminology.

Practical Methods for Categorization and Tagging

Microsoft Lists empowers users with intuitive tools for implementing categorization and tagging effectively. Explore practical methods and workflows tailored to optimize organizational efficiency:

1. Creating Custom Views

Custom views enable users to tailor list displays based on specific categories or tags. Configure filters and sorting criteria to customize views that align with distinct project phases, priorities, or user preferences. This feature enhances usability by presenting relevant information in contextually meaningful formats.

2. Utilizing Metadata Columns

Metadata columns serve as dynamic attributes that enrich list items with contextual information. Leverage metadata to capture and classify data attributes such as status, priority, or departmental affiliations. This structured approach enhances data organization and facilitates comprehensive analysis and reporting.

3. Integrating with Microsoft 365 Ecosystem

Harness the interoperability of Microsoft Lists with other Microsoft 365 applications to amplify categorization and tagging capabilities. Seamlessly integrate lists with Microsoft

Teams, SharePoint, and Power Automate to leverage advanced functionalities for enhanced data management and workflow automation.

Best Practices for Effective Categorization and Tagging

Implementing best practices ensures the efficacy and sustainability of categorization and tagging strategies within Microsoft Lists. Adopt the following guidelines to optimize organizational efficiency and maximize the benefits of structured data management:

1. Establish Clear Guidelines

Define clear guidelines and standards for categorization and tagging practices. Document best practices, naming conventions, and taxonomy structures to foster consistency and mitigate potential ambiguities or redundancies.

2. Regular Maintenance and Review

Regularly review and refine categorization and tagging frameworks to adapt to evolving organizational requirements and project dynamics. Conduct periodic audits to validate the relevance and accuracy of categories and tags, ensuring alignment with current operational objectives.

3. Training and Awareness

Promote user proficiency through training initiatives that emphasize the importance of effective categorization and tagging. Educate team members on utilizing advanced features and optimizing workflows to maximize productivity and collaboration within Microsoft Lists.

Conclusion

Categorizing and tagging lists within Microsoft Lists represents a pivotal strategy for optimizing data organization and enhancing operational efficiency. By implementing structured categorization frameworks, leveraging robust tagging capabilities, and adhering to best practices, organizations can streamline information management processes and empower teams to achieve heightened productivity and collaboration.

7.2 Maintaining Data Integrity

Regular Data Audits

Ensuring the integrity of data within Microsoft Lists is crucial for maintaining accuracy, compliance, and trustworthiness. Regular data audits play a pivotal role in achieving these objectives. This section explores the importance of data audits, best practices for conducting them effectively, and the tools available within Microsoft Lists to streamline this process.

Importance of Data Audits

Data audits serve as a proactive measure to identify and rectify inaccuracies, inconsistencies, or anomalies within datasets stored in Microsoft Lists. By systematically reviewing data on a regular basis, organizations can mitigate risks associated with erroneous information, ensure regulatory compliance, and uphold data quality standards. Moreover, audits contribute to enhancing decision-making processes by providing reliable and up-to-date insights.

Best Practices for Conducting Data Audits

Successful data audits require careful planning, execution, and follow-up actions. Below are essential best practices to consider:

1. Establish Clear Objectives and Scope: Define the goals of the audit, including specific datasets, fields, and criteria to be reviewed. This ensures focus and clarity throughout the auditing process.

2. Create Audit Checklists: Develop standardized checklists outlining audit procedures, data validation rules, and compliance requirements. Checklists help auditors systematically review data and maintain consistency across audits.

3. Utilize Data Sampling Techniques: Depending on the volume of data, employ sampling techniques to assess data subsets efficiently. Random and stratified sampling methods provide statistically valid insights without overwhelming audit resources.

4. Verify Data Accuracy and Completeness: Validate data entries against predefined standards, such as formatting guidelines, mandatory fields, and permissible values. Identify missing, outdated, or duplicated records that may compromise data integrity.

5. Assess Data Security Measures: Evaluate the adequacy of data security protocols implemented within Microsoft Lists. Review access controls, encryption practices, and audit trails to safeguard sensitive information against unauthorized access or breaches.

6. Document Findings and Recommendations: Document audit findings, including identified discrepancies, observations, and recommendations for corrective actions. Maintain comprehensive records to track audit outcomes and monitor progress over time.

7. Collaborate with Stakeholders: Engage stakeholders, including data owners, IT administrators, and compliance officers, throughout the audit process. Foster collaboration to address identified issues promptly and implement necessary improvements.

Tools and Features in Microsoft Lists

Microsoft Lists offers robust tools and features to facilitate efficient data auditing processes:

- Column Validation: Define validation rules within list columns to enforce data integrity, such as required fields, date ranges, or unique values.

- Flow Integration: Automate audit workflows using Microsoft Power Automate to schedule recurring audits, notify stakeholders of audit results, and trigger follow-up actions based on predefined conditions.

- Version History: Track changes made to list items over time, allowing auditors to review previous versions, restore data if necessary, and maintain an audit trail for compliance purposes.

- Data Export and Analysis: Export list data to Microsoft Excel for in-depth analysis, trend identification, and visualization of audit findings. Leverage Excel's advanced features to perform complex data comparisons and trend analyses.

Case Study: Implementing Data Audits in a Corporate Environment

To illustrate the practical application of data audits within Microsoft Lists, consider a case study of a multinational corporation implementing stringent data governance practices. This corporation utilizes Microsoft Lists to manage vendor relationships and procurement processes across its global operations. By conducting regular data audits, the corporation ensures that vendor information, pricing agreements, and contractual terms remain accurate and compliant with regulatory standards.

The audit process involves:

- Reviewing vendor records for completeness and accuracy, including contact details, financial information, and contract expiration dates.

- Validating procurement transactions against predefined budgetary limits and approval workflows.

- Assessing data security measures to protect confidential vendor information from unauthorized access or data breaches.

Through proactive data auditing, the corporation identifies discrepancies, mitigates operational risks, and enhances transparency in vendor management practices. Continuous improvement initiatives, guided by audit findings, enable the corporation to optimize procurement efficiencies and maintain trust with stakeholders.

Conclusion

In conclusion, regular data audits are indispensable for ensuring data integrity, regulatory compliance, and informed decision-making within Microsoft Lists. By adhering to best practices, leveraging advanced audit tools, and implementing case-specific strategies, organizations can fortify their data governance frameworks and sustain high standards of data quality and reliability. Embracing a proactive approach to data auditing empowers organizations to harness the full potential of Microsoft Lists as a robust platform for data-driven insights and operational excellence.

Implementing Data Security Measures

Ensuring data security within Microsoft Lists is paramount to maintaining trust and compliance with organizational standards. Implementing robust data security measures involves a comprehensive approach that addresses both technical aspects and user behaviors. This section explores various strategies and best practices for safeguarding data integrity within Microsoft Lists.

Understanding Data Security in Microsoft Lists

Data security in Microsoft Lists revolves around protecting sensitive information from unauthorized access, modification, or loss. As organizations increasingly rely on digital platforms for data management, implementing effective security measures becomes crucial to mitigate risks associated with data breaches and compliance violations.

Key Components of Data Security Measures

1. Authentication and Access Control

Ensuring proper authentication mechanisms and access controls is fundamental to preventing unauthorized access to sensitive data. Microsoft Lists integrates with Azure Active Directory (Azure AD), enabling organizations to enforce multi-factor authentication (MFA), role-based access control (RBAC), and conditional access policies. By configuring these settings, administrators can restrict access based on user roles, locations, or device compliance, thereby fortifying data security at the authentication layer.

2. Encryption of Data at Rest and in Transit

Encrypting data both at rest and in transit adds an additional layer of protection against data breaches. Microsoft Lists employs industry-standard encryption protocols, such as

Transport Layer Security (TLS) for data in transit and BitLocker encryption for data at rest within Microsoft 365 environments. Organizations should ensure that encryption settings are enabled and configured appropriately to safeguard data integrity across all communication channels and storage repositories.

3. Data Loss Prevention (DLP) Policies

Implementing Data Loss Prevention (DLP) policies helps organizations proactively identify, monitor, and protect sensitive information within Microsoft Lists. DLP policies can be configured to automatically detect and classify sensitive data, such as personally identifiable information (PII) or financial records, and apply actions, such as encryption or restriction of sharing, to prevent inadvertent data leakage. Organizations can customize DLP policies to align with regulatory requirements and internal data protection policies, thereby fostering a secure data environment.

4. Audit Logging and Monitoring

Enabling audit logging and continuous monitoring of user activities within Microsoft Lists provides visibility into data access patterns and potential security incidents. Microsoft 365 Security & Compliance Center offers robust auditing capabilities that track user actions, changes to list configurations, and access attempts. By reviewing audit logs regularly, organizations can detect suspicious activities, unauthorized access attempts, or policy violations, enabling timely response and mitigation of security risks.

Best Practices for Implementing Data Security Measures

1. Conduct Regular Security Assessments

Periodically assessing and auditing data security measures ensures that they remain effective against evolving threats and compliance requirements. Conducting vulnerability assessments, penetration testing, and security audits help identify gaps or vulnerabilities in the implementation of data security controls within Microsoft Lists. Organizations should establish a schedule for regular security assessments and allocate resources to address identified risks promptly.

2. Educate Users on Security Best Practices

Promoting a culture of security awareness among users is essential for maintaining data integrity in Microsoft Lists. Educate users on recognizing phishing attempts, adhering to password policies, and securely sharing information within lists. Provide training sessions or workshops that emphasize the importance of data security measures and encourage proactive participation in maintaining a secure digital environment.

3. Implement Data Retention and Disposal Policies

Establishing data retention and disposal policies ensures that outdated or redundant information stored in Microsoft Lists is managed securely and in compliance with regulatory requirements. Define retention periods for different types of data within lists and automate retention policies using Microsoft 365 Compliance Center. Implement procedures for securely deleting or archiving data that has reached the end of its retention period, minimizing the risk of unauthorized access or data exposure.

4. Monitor Security Alerts and Incident Response

Maintaining vigilance through proactive monitoring of security alerts and incident response procedures enhances the organization's ability to detect and respond to potential security incidents in Microsoft Lists. Configure alerts for suspicious activities, unauthorized access attempts, or policy violations within Microsoft 365 Security & Compliance Center. Establish incident response protocols that outline roles, responsibilities, and escalation procedures for addressing security breaches or data breaches promptly and effectively.

Conclusion

Implementing effective data security measures within Microsoft Lists is essential for safeguarding sensitive information, maintaining regulatory compliance, and fostering trust among users and stakeholders. By integrating authentication controls, encryption protocols, DLP policies, and proactive monitoring practices, organizations can mitigate risks associated with data breaches and ensure the integrity and confidentiality of data stored in Microsoft Lists.

7.3 Tips for Efficient Workflow

Keyboard Shortcuts

Keyboard shortcuts are invaluable tools for improving productivity and efficiency when working with Microsoft Lists. By mastering these shortcuts, users can perform tasks more quickly, navigate the interface with ease, and streamline their workflow. This section explores a comprehensive list of keyboard shortcuts available in Microsoft Lists and provides practical examples of how to integrate them into daily use.

Introduction to Keyboard Shortcuts

Keyboard shortcuts are key combinations that allow users to perform tasks without needing to navigate through menus or use a mouse extensively. They are designed to save time, minimize repetitive actions, and enhance the overall user experience. Microsoft Lists supports a wide range of keyboard shortcuts across various functionalities, empowering users to accomplish tasks more efficiently.

Basic Navigation and List Management

Understanding basic navigation shortcuts is fundamental to efficiently maneuvering through Microsoft Lists. For instance, using **Ctrl + N** to create a new list or **Ctrl + S** to save changes can significantly reduce the time spent on routine actions. Navigational shortcuts also include **Ctrl + Arrow keys** for moving between cells and **Tab** for quick navigation within forms and fields.

Editing and Formatting Shortcuts

Efficient editing and formatting are essential for maintaining clarity and consistency in lists. Keyboard shortcuts such as **Ctrl + C** for copying, **Ctrl + V** for pasting, and **Ctrl + X** for cutting data streamline content manipulation. These shortcuts are complemented by formatting commands like **Ctrl + B** for bold, **Ctrl + I** for italic, and **Ctrl + U** for underline, ensuring that data is presented in a clear and structured manner.

Selection and Navigation Shortcuts

Managing large datasets requires precise selection and navigation techniques. Shortcut combinations like **Ctrl + A** to select all items, **Ctrl + Space** to select entire columns, and **Shift + Arrow keys** for extending selection boundaries facilitate efficient data handling. These shortcuts empower users to quickly highlight relevant information and expedite decision-making processes.

Task and Workflow Automation Shortcuts

Automation is key to optimizing workflow efficiency within Microsoft Lists. Keyboard shortcuts such as **Ctrl + D** for duplicating items, **Ctrl + E** for editing items inline, and **Ctrl + P** for printing lists accelerate routine tasks. Advanced automation shortcuts, including **Ctrl + Shift + F** for applying filters and **Ctrl + Shift + L** for toggling column totals, further enhance productivity by automating complex data manipulations.

Integration with Other Microsoft 365 Apps

Seamless integration with other Microsoft 365 applications is facilitated through intuitive keyboard shortcuts. For instance, using **Alt + Tab** to switch between open applications or **Ctrl + Shift + M** to create a new list item from an Outlook email enhances cross-platform connectivity. These shortcuts enable users to leverage the full potential of Microsoft Lists within a unified productivity ecosystem.

Customization and Personalization Shortcuts

Tailoring Microsoft Lists to meet specific user preferences is simplified through customization shortcuts. Keyboard combinations such as **Alt + H, I, T** to insert a new column or **Alt + H, O, T** to sort list data alphabetically empower users to personalize their workspace effortlessly. These shortcuts facilitate quick adjustments to list layouts and configurations, ensuring optimal usability and efficiency.

Accessibility and Usability Enhancements

Enhancing accessibility and usability is crucial for accommodating diverse user needs within Microsoft Lists. Keyboard shortcuts, including **Alt + Shift + F10** to access the context menu or **Alt + N, O** to open list options, promote inclusivity by providing alternative navigation methods. These shortcuts foster a more intuitive user experience and enable efficient interaction with lists across various devices and environments.

Practical Application and Implementation

Implementing keyboard shortcuts effectively requires practice and familiarity with Microsoft Lists' interface and functionalities. By incorporating these shortcuts into daily workflows, users can gradually increase their productivity and proficiency. Practical examples, such as creating a list template with **Ctrl + Shift + O** or navigating between list items with **Up** and **Down** arrows, demonstrate the practical application of shortcuts in real-world scenarios.

Conclusion

Keyboard shortcuts represent a cornerstone of efficient workflow management within Microsoft Lists. By mastering these shortcuts, users can streamline navigation, enhance data management capabilities, and optimize productivity. Continuous exploration and utilization of keyboard shortcuts empower users to maximize their efficiency and derive greater value from Microsoft Lists as a comprehensive organizational tool.

Time-Saving Tips and Tricks

In the fast-paced world of business, efficiency is key. Microsoft Lists offers a variety of features and shortcuts that can significantly improve your workflow and save you precious time. By leveraging these tips and tricks, you can streamline your processes, reduce manual work, and enhance overall productivity. Below, we delve into some practical strategies to help you get the most out of Microsoft Lists.

1. Utilize Templates for Quick List Creation

Microsoft Lists provides a range of pre-built templates tailored to various business needs. Using these templates can save you the time and effort of setting up lists from scratch. Templates are available for tasks such as issue tracking, project management, event itinerary, and more.

- How to Use Templates: When creating a new list, choose from the available templates in the gallery. Each template comes with predefined columns and settings, which you can customize further to fit your specific requirements.

2. Employ Conditional Formatting for Visual Cues

Conditional formatting allows you to highlight important information or trends in your lists. By setting up rules that change the appearance of list items based on certain criteria, you can quickly identify critical data without manually sifting through rows and columns.

- Setting Up Conditional Formatting: Navigate to the list settings and select 'Format current view.' From there, you can add conditional formatting rules to change the color, font style, or background of list items that meet specific conditions.

3. Leverage Quick Edit Mode for Bulk Changes

Quick Edit mode (also known as "Grid view") is a powerful feature for making bulk changes to your list items. This mode transforms your list into a spreadsheet-like interface, allowing you to edit multiple items at once, copy and paste data, and use keyboard shortcuts for faster navigation.

- Activating Quick Edit Mode: Open your list and select the 'Quick Edit' button on the toolbar. This will switch your list into Grid view, where you can easily make multiple changes.

4. Create Custom Views to Focus on Relevant Data

Custom views enable you to display only the information that is most relevant to you. By setting up different views with specific filters, sorting, and grouping, you can quickly access the data you need without being overwhelmed by unnecessary details.

- Creating Custom Views: In the list settings, select 'Create view.' You can then define the columns to display, apply filters, and set up sorting and grouping options. Save the view for future use and switch between views as needed.

5. Automate Repetitive Tasks with Power Automate

Microsoft Power Automate (formerly Microsoft Flow) allows you to create automated workflows that connect Microsoft Lists with other apps and services. By automating repetitive tasks, you can reduce manual work and ensure consistency in your processes.

- Example Automations: Set up a flow to send email notifications when a new item is added to a list, automatically move items to another list based on specific criteria, or synchronize data between Microsoft Lists and other applications like SharePoint or Teams.

6. Use Filters and Sorting for On-the-Fly Data Analysis

Filters and sorting options are invaluable for quickly analyzing your data. By applying filters, you can narrow down the list items to those that meet specific criteria. Sorting allows you to organize the data in ascending or descending order based on any column.

- Applying Filters and Sorting: Use the column headers in your list to apply filters and sorting. Click on a column header to access the filter and sort options. You can also combine multiple filters to refine your data further.

7. Implement Calculated Columns for Dynamic Data

Calculated columns enable you to perform calculations and display the results directly in your list. This can be useful for tasks such as totaling amounts, calculating dates, or generating custom values based on other columns.

- Creating Calculated Columns: In the list settings, add a new column and select 'Calculated (calculation based on other columns).' Define the formula you want to use, and the calculated column will display the results automatically.

8. Take Advantage of Keyboard Shortcuts

Keyboard shortcuts can significantly speed up your workflow by allowing you to perform common actions without using the mouse. Microsoft Lists supports a variety of shortcuts for tasks such as navigating the interface, editing items, and more.

- Common Keyboard Shortcuts:

  - `Ctrl + N`: Create a new list item.

  - `Ctrl + S`: Save changes to a list item.

  - `Ctrl + E`: Open the Quick Edit mode.

  - `Ctrl + Shift + F`: Open the filter pane.

  - `Ctrl + F`: Search within the list.

9. Customize Forms with Power Apps

Microsoft Power Apps allows you to create custom forms for your lists. By customizing forms, you can provide a more user-friendly interface for data entry, include validation rules, and ensure that all necessary information is captured accurately.

- Creating Custom Forms: From your list, select 'Integrate' and then 'Power Apps.' Choose 'Customize forms' to open Power Apps and start designing your custom form. You can add controls, set validation rules, and format the form to meet your needs.

10. Use the Microsoft Lists Mobile App for On-the-Go Access

The Microsoft Lists mobile app provides access to your lists from your mobile device. This is especially useful for field workers or team members who need to update or view list items while away from their desks.

- Mobile App Features: The mobile app supports all the core functionality of Microsoft Lists, including viewing, editing, and creating list items. It also allows you to access shared lists and use offline mode for working without an internet connection.

11. Implement Effective Permissions Management

Managing permissions effectively ensures that the right people have access to the right data. By setting up permissions correctly, you can prevent unauthorized access and maintain data security.

- Setting Permissions: In the list settings, navigate to 'Permissions for this list.' From there, you can grant or restrict access to individual users or groups, and set specific permissions for viewing, editing, or managing the list.

12. Use Recurrence for Regular Tasks

If you have tasks that recur on a regular basis, you can set up recurring items in Microsoft Lists. This can be particularly useful for tracking maintenance schedules, routine check-ups, or periodic reviews.

- Setting Up Recurrence: When creating a new list item, look for the recurrence option (if supported by your list template). Define the recurrence pattern, such as daily, weekly, or monthly, and Microsoft Lists will automatically generate the recurring items.

13. Organize Lists with Folders and Grouping

Folders and grouping options help you organize your list items in a structured way. By using folders, you can categorize items into different sections. Grouping allows you to visually separate items based on a specific column.

- Creating Folders: In the list settings, enable folders if they are not already enabled. Create new folders and move items into them as needed.

- Grouping Items: In the list view settings, select 'Group by' and choose the column you want to group items by. This will organize your list items into expandable and collapsible groups based on the selected column.

14. Regularly Review and Clean Up Lists

Over time, lists can become cluttered with outdated or irrelevant items. Regularly reviewing and cleaning up your lists helps maintain their usefulness and accuracy.

- Reviewing Lists: Set a schedule for periodically reviewing your lists. Look for items that are no longer needed, duplicates, or inaccuracies.

- Cleaning Up: Remove or archive outdated items, correct any errors, and ensure that the list structure still meets your needs.

Conclusion

By implementing these time-saving tips and tricks, you can make your workflow in Microsoft Lists more efficient and effective. The key to mastering Microsoft Lists lies in understanding its features and applying best practices to suit your specific needs. Whether you are managing projects, tracking tasks, or organizing data, these strategies will help you work smarter, not harder. Embrace the full potential of Microsoft Lists and enjoy the benefits of a streamlined, organized, and productive workflow.

CHAPTER VIII
Troubleshooting and Support

8.1 Common Issues and Solutions

Data import issues can be a significant roadblock for users looking to leverage Microsoft Lists for efficient data management. This section will delve into common problems encountered during data import and provide comprehensive solutions to address these issues effectively.

Troubleshooting Data Import Problems

Data import problems can arise due to various factors, such as incorrect file formats, data inconsistencies, or technical glitches. To help you overcome these challenges, we will explore the following areas:

1. Understanding Supported File Formats

2. Preparing Your Data for Import

3. Resolving Data Format Issues

4. Handling Large Data Sets

5. Addressing Permissions and Access Issues

6. Using Import Tools and Options

7. Troubleshooting Common Errors

---

1. Understanding Supported File Formats

Before importing data into Microsoft Lists, it's crucial to understand the supported file formats. Microsoft Lists primarily supports data imports from:

- Excel Files (.xlsx, .xls): Excel is the most commonly used format for importing data into Microsoft Lists. Ensure your Excel files are properly formatted and contain the data you need to import.

- CSV Files (.csv): Comma-separated values (CSV) files are another supported format. These files are text files with data fields separated by commas, making them easy to use for data transfer.

- Text Files (.txt): While less common, text files can also be used for data import. Ensure the data is structured correctly, with fields separated by tabs or commas.

Knowing the supported formats allows you to prepare your data correctly, minimizing the risk of import errors.

---

 2. Preparing Your Data for Import

Proper data preparation is crucial for a successful import process. Here are some steps to prepare your data effectively:

- Clean Your Data: Ensure that your data is free of errors, duplicates, and inconsistencies. Clean data will import more smoothly and reduce the likelihood of issues.

- Use Consistent Formatting: Standardize data formats across your file. For example, ensure dates are in the same format, and numeric values are consistent.

- Remove Unnecessary Data: Eliminate any data that is not required for your list. This will simplify the import process and reduce the chance of errors.

- Check for Blank Rows and Columns: Blank rows and columns can cause issues during import. Remove them to ensure a smooth import process.

- Validate Data: Use Excel's data validation tools to check for errors and inconsistencies in your data before importing.

---

 3. Resolving Data Format Issues

Data format issues are common during the import process. Here are some tips to resolve these issues:

- Date Formats: Ensure that all dates are in a consistent format, such as MM/DD/YYYY or DD/MM/YYYY. Mixed date formats can cause import errors.

- Numeric Data: Check that numeric data is free of symbols (e.g., $, %, etc.) and is formatted consistently. Convert text-based numbers to numeric format if necessary.

- Text Data: Ensure that text data is consistent in terms of capitalization, spelling, and spacing. Use Excel's find and replace feature to standardize text data.

- Special Characters: Remove or replace special characters that might cause issues during import. This includes symbols like &, %, and .

---

4. Handling Large Data Sets

Importing large data sets can be challenging due to size limitations and performance issues. Here are some strategies to handle large data imports:

- Split Large Files: If your data file is too large, consider splitting it into smaller files and importing them separately. This can help avoid performance issues and reduce the risk of import errors.

- Use Batch Imports: Import your data in batches instead of all at once. This can help manage system resources and prevent timeouts or crashes.

- Optimize Your Data: Remove any unnecessary data and optimize your file to reduce its size. This includes removing blank rows and columns, as well as unnecessary formatting.

- Check System Resources: Ensure your system has adequate resources (e.g., memory, processing power) to handle large data imports. Close any unnecessary applications to free up resources.

---

5. Addressing Permissions and Access Issues

Permissions and access issues can prevent successful data imports. Here's how to address these problems:

- Check User Permissions: Ensure you have the necessary permissions to import data into the target list. This includes read and write access.

- Verify List Settings: Check the settings of the target list to ensure it allows data imports. This includes verifying list permissions and any restrictions on data imports.

- Contact IT Support: If you encounter persistent permission issues, contact your IT support team for assistance. They can help resolve access issues and ensure you have the necessary permissions.

---

6. Using Import Tools and Options

Microsoft Lists provides various tools and options to facilitate data import. Here's how to use them effectively:

- Excel Import Wizard: Use the Excel import wizard to guide you through the data import process. This tool helps map Excel columns to list columns and provides options to resolve data issues.

- Power Automate: Use Power Automate to create automated workflows for data import. This tool allows you to automate repetitive tasks and streamline the import process.

- Third-Party Tools: Consider using third-party tools and plugins to facilitate data import. These tools often provide additional features and options for managing data imports.

---

7. Troubleshooting Common Errors

Despite best efforts, you may encounter errors during the data import process. Here's how to troubleshoot common errors:

- Import Error Messages: Review any error messages provided during the import process. These messages often provide insights into the cause of the error and how to resolve it.

- Data Mapping Issues: Ensure that Excel columns are correctly mapped to list columns. Incorrect mappings can cause data import errors.

- File Format Errors: Verify that your file format is supported and correctly structured. Unsupported or incorrectly formatted files can cause import errors.

- Data Size Limits: Check for any size limits on data imports and ensure your file does not exceed these limits. Split large files if necessary.

Conclusion

Troubleshooting data import problems in Microsoft Lists requires a methodical approach. By understanding supported file formats, preparing your data, resolving format issues, handling large data sets, addressing permissions, using import tools, and troubleshooting common errors, you can ensure a smooth and successful data import process. Implement these strategies to overcome data import challenges and make the most of Microsoft Lists for efficient data management.

Fixing Access and Permission Issues

Access and permission issues are common hurdles users encounter when working with Microsoft Lists. These issues can arise from a variety of factors, including improper configuration of permissions, changes in user roles, or system updates. Addressing these challenges effectively is crucial for maintaining smooth operations and ensuring data security. In this section, we will explore various scenarios where access and permission issues might arise, discuss the underlying causes, and provide step-by-step solutions to resolve these problems.

Understanding Microsoft Lists Permissions

Before diving into specific issues and solutions, it is essential to understand the permission model used by Microsoft Lists. Permissions in Microsoft Lists are managed through SharePoint, as Lists are built on the SharePoint platform. The permission levels can be configured at the site level, list level, and even at the item level. The key permission levels include:

- Full Control: Users can manage site settings, permissions, and all list content.

- Design: Users can create lists and document libraries, edit pages, and apply themes.

- Edit: Users can add, edit, and delete items in lists and libraries.

- Contribute: Users can add and edit items in existing lists and libraries.

- Read: Users can view items and pages.

- Limited Access: Users can access specific items without full access to the entire list or site.

Permissions can be customized further by creating unique permission levels or breaking inheritance to apply different permissions to specific lists or items.

Common Access and Permission Issues

1. Users Unable to Access a List

2. Users Unable to Edit or Add Items

3. Users Seeing Limited Information

4. Users Receiving Access Denied Errors

5. Permission Changes Not Taking Effect

Let's delve into each of these issues, identify potential causes, and outline the steps to resolve them.

1. Users Unable to Access a List

Scenario: A user reports that they cannot access a specific list, even though they should have the necessary permissions.

Potential Causes:

- The user is not a member of the site or group with access to the list.

- Permissions inheritance has been broken, and the list has unique permissions that do not include the user.

- The user's permissions were accidentally removed or modified.

Solution:

Step 1: Verify User Membership

- Navigate to the SharePoint site where the list is located.

- Go to "Site Settings" and select "People and groups" under the "Users and Permissions" section.

- Ensure the user is a member of a group that has access to the site.

Step 2: Check List Permissions

- Go to the list and select "List Settings" from the settings menu.

- Under "Permissions and Management," select "Permissions for this list."

- Verify if the list inherits permissions from the parent site or has unique permissions.

- If the list has unique permissions, ensure the user or a group the user belongs to has been granted access.

Step 3: Restore Inheritance or Adjust Permissions

- If permissions inheritance was broken, consider restoring inheritance if appropriate. Select "Inherit Permissions" to apply the site's permissions to the list.

- Alternatively, add the user directly to the list permissions or to a group with the necessary access.

 2. Users Unable to Edit or Add Items

Scenario: Users can view a list but are unable to add or edit items within it.

Potential Causes:

- The user has read-only permissions.

- The list settings restrict editing or adding items.

- Content approval settings are enabled, and the user does not have approval permissions.

Solution:

Step 1: Verify User Permissions

- Go to "List Settings" and select "Permissions for this list."

- Ensure the user or group has "Contribute" or higher permission level.

Step 2: Check List Settings

- In "List Settings," review the "Advanced settings" section.

- Ensure that item-level permissions allow users to create and edit all items or only their own items, based on the requirements.

Step 3: Review Content Approval Settings

- If content approval is enabled, check the user's role in the approval process.

- Go to "List Settings" and select "Versioning settings."

- Ensure the user has the necessary permissions to submit items for approval or approve items if required.

3. Users Seeing Limited Information

Scenario: A user can access the list but only sees limited information or certain columns are hidden.

Potential Causes:

- Column-level permissions or view-level permissions are restricting access.

- Custom views are applied that do not include all columns.

- Personal views are in use, and the user has not included all columns in their view.

Solution:

Step 1: Check Column-Level Permissions

- Navigate to "List Settings" and select "Column settings."

- Ensure that there are no column-level permissions restricting visibility.

Step 2: Review and Modify List Views

- Go to the list and select the current view from the view selector dropdown.

- Click "Edit current view" to modify the columns included in the view.

- Ensure all necessary columns are selected and visible in the view.

Step 3: Adjust Personal Views

- Instruct the user to check if they are using a personal view.

- If so, they should modify their personal view to include the required columns by following similar steps as above.

4. Users Receiving Access Denied Errors

Scenario: Users are encountering "Access Denied" errors when attempting to access a list or specific items within a list.

Potential Causes:

- The user does not have the necessary permissions.

- The user's permissions were accidentally revoked or not properly granted.

- The list or item has unique permissions that do not include the user.

Solution:

Step 1: Verify User Permissions

- Navigate to the list and go to "List Settings."

- Select "Permissions for this list" and verify the user's permissions.

- If necessary, add the user or group with appropriate permissions.

Step 2: Check Item-Level Permissions

- If the error occurs for specific items, check if those items have unique permissions.

- Select the item, click on "Item" from the ribbon, and then "Shared With."

- Adjust item-level permissions to include the user or group.

Step 3: Restore or Adjust Permissions

- If unique permissions are not needed, restore inheritance to apply list permissions to all items.

- Alternatively, adjust permissions at the item level to grant the necessary access.

5. Permission Changes Not Taking Effect

Scenario: Changes made to permissions do not seem to take effect immediately or at all.

Potential Causes:

- There may be a delay in the system updating permissions.

- Browser cache or cookies may be causing issues.

- Permissions changes were not applied correctly or completely.

Solution:

Step 1: Allow Time for Updates

- After making changes, wait for a few minutes and ask the user to retry accessing the list or item.

Step 2: Clear Browser Cache and Cookies

- Instruct the user to clear their browser cache and cookies.

- Have the user log out and log back into the SharePoint site.

Step 3: Reapply Permissions

- Go to "List Settings" and verify the permissions.

- If necessary, reapply the permissions to ensure all changes are correctly implemented.

- Consider breaking and then re-establishing inheritance if permissions were not correctly updated.

Best Practices for Managing Permissions

To minimize access and permission issues, consider adopting the following best practices:

- Regularly Review Permissions: Periodically review permissions for your SharePoint site and lists to ensure they align with current user roles and responsibilities.

- Use Groups Instead of Individual Users: Assign permissions to groups rather than individual users. This simplifies management and reduces the likelihood of errors when permissions need to be updated.

- Document Permission Changes: Keep a log of permission changes, including who made the change, when it was made, and the reason for the change. This can help with troubleshooting and auditing.

- Educate Users: Provide training and resources to users on how permissions work in SharePoint and Microsoft Lists. This can help users understand the importance of permissions and avoid accidental changes.

By understanding the permission model, identifying common issues, and applying best practices, you can effectively manage access and permissions in Microsoft Lists. This ensures that users have the appropriate level of access to perform their tasks while maintaining the security and integrity of your data.

8.2 Accessing Help and Support

Accessing support and resources is crucial for effectively utilizing Microsoft Lists and overcoming any challenges that may arise. Microsoft provides a comprehensive suite of support options and resources designed to assist users in navigating and resolving issues. This section will delve into the various support resources available from Microsoft, ensuring you can leverage them to maximize your efficiency and productivity with Microsoft Lists.

Using Microsoft's Support Resources

Microsoft offers a wide array of support resources to help users of all levels—from beginners to advanced professionals—resolve issues and enhance their experience with Microsoft Lists. These resources include online documentation, community forums, direct support channels, training materials, and more. Let's explore these resources in detail.

1. Microsoft Support Website

The Microsoft Support website is the primary hub for all things related to Microsoft product support. It offers a wealth of information, including articles, guides, FAQs, and troubleshooting tips. Here's how to make the most of it:

- Navigation and Search: The support website is user-friendly and features a robust search function. Simply type in keywords related to your issue or question, and you will be presented with a list of relevant articles and resources.

- Topics and Categories: The site is organized into various topics and categories. For Microsoft Lists, you can navigate to the Office 365 section or directly search for "Microsoft Lists" to find targeted resources.

- Step-by-Step Guides: Many articles provide step-by-step guides to resolving common issues or performing specific tasks. These guides are detailed and often include screenshots to aid understanding.

- FAQs and Common Issues: The FAQ sections are particularly useful for quick answers to common problems. Reviewing these can save time if your issue is a known one with a straightforward solution.

2. Microsoft Docs

Microsoft Docs is another valuable resource, especially for more technical users or those looking to deeply understand Microsoft Lists' functionalities. Microsoft Docs provides in-depth documentation and technical guides. Here's how to utilize it:

- Comprehensive Documentation: Microsoft Docs offers comprehensive documentation on Microsoft Lists, covering everything from basic usage to advanced features and integrations. This documentation is continuously updated to reflect the latest features and best practices.

- Code Samples and API References: For developers, Microsoft Docs includes code samples and API references. This is particularly useful if you are looking to integrate Microsoft Lists with other applications or customize its functionality through scripting and automation.

- Learning Paths: Microsoft Docs also features learning paths, which are structured modules designed to teach specific skills or concepts. For example, there may be a learning path dedicated to mastering Microsoft Lists, guiding users through various aspects from beginner to advanced levels.

3. Microsoft Learn

Microsoft Learn is an interactive learning platform that provides free, self-paced learning experiences. It includes tutorials, interactive labs, and certifications. Here's how it can help with Microsoft Lists:

- Learning Modules: Microsoft Learn offers learning modules specific to Microsoft Lists and other Office 365 applications. These modules are interactive and often include hands-on labs to practice what you've learned.

- Certification Programs: If you want to demonstrate your proficiency, consider pursuing a Microsoft certification. Microsoft Learn provides resources and preparation materials for certifications related to Office 365 and Microsoft Lists.

- Interactive Labs: The interactive labs allow you to work in a virtual environment where you can practice using Microsoft Lists without affecting your actual data or setup. This is a safe way to experiment and learn.

4. Microsoft Community Forums

The Microsoft Community Forums are a vibrant place to connect with other users, share experiences, and seek help. Here's how to effectively use the forums:

- Asking Questions: You can post questions about any issues or uncertainties you have regarding Microsoft Lists. The community includes both Microsoft experts and experienced users who can provide helpful responses.

- Searching for Answers: Before posting a new question, it's a good idea to search the forums. Often, someone else may have had the same issue, and there might already be a solution posted.

- Participating in Discussions: Engaging in discussions not only helps you solve your issues but also enhances your understanding by reading about others' experiences and solutions.

5. Microsoft Tech Community

The Microsoft Tech Community is another platform where IT professionals and developers can find and share information about Microsoft products, including Microsoft Lists. Here's what it offers:

- Blog Posts and Articles: The Tech Community includes blog posts and articles written by Microsoft experts and community members. These posts often cover new features, best practices, and troubleshooting tips.

- Webinars and Events: The community frequently hosts webinars and virtual events. Attending these can provide deeper insights and live demonstrations of Microsoft Lists features.

- Discussion Spaces: Similar to the community forums, the Tech Community has dedicated discussion spaces where you can ask questions and engage with other users.

6. Microsoft Support App

For on-the-go support, the Microsoft Support app provides access to many of the same resources available on the website. It's particularly useful for quick troubleshooting or checking the status of a support request.

- Easy Access: Download the Microsoft Support app on your mobile device for easy access to support articles, FAQs, and contact options.

- Real-Time Assistance: The app allows you to contact support directly from your mobile device, making it convenient to get help when you need it.

7. Contacting Microsoft Support

When self-help resources are not enough, you may need to contact Microsoft Support directly. Here's how to do it:

- Live Chat: Microsoft offers a live chat option where you can interact with a support agent in real-time. This is useful for immediate assistance.

- Phone Support: For more complex issues, phone support might be necessary. Microsoft provides phone numbers for different regions and product-specific support lines.

- Email Support: If your issue is not urgent, you can also email Microsoft Support. This option is suitable for problems that require detailed explanations and do not need immediate resolution.

- Support Tickets: For enterprise users or more critical issues, submitting a support ticket through the Microsoft Admin Center might be the best route. This allows you to track the status of your request and ensure it is handled promptly.

8. Microsoft Virtual Agent

The Microsoft Virtual Agent is an AI-powered tool designed to provide quick answers to common questions. Here's how to use it:

- Chat Interface: The virtual agent operates through a chat interface, where you can type questions and receive instant responses.

- Guided Solutions: It can guide you through troubleshooting steps and provide links to relevant articles and resources.

- 24/7 Availability: The virtual agent is available 24/7, making it a convenient option for support outside of regular business hours.

9. Training and Workshops

Microsoft offers various training sessions and workshops that can help you get the most out of Microsoft Lists. These sessions range from beginner to advanced levels and cover a wide array of topics.

- Online Training Sessions: Microsoft regularly hosts online training sessions that you can attend from the comfort of your home or office. These sessions often include live demonstrations and Q&A segments.

- In-Person Workshops: Depending on your location, you might have the opportunity to attend in-person workshops. These workshops provide hands-on experience and direct interaction with trainers.

- Customized Training: For businesses and organizations, Microsoft offers customized training sessions tailored to the specific needs of your team. These can be especially useful for ensuring all members are proficient with Microsoft Lists.

10. Microsoft Partners

Microsoft Partners are certified experts who can provide additional support and consulting services. Here's how they can help:

- Consulting Services: Partners can offer consulting services to help you implement Microsoft Lists effectively within your organization. They can assist with setup, customization, and optimization.

- Technical Support: In addition to Microsoft's direct support, partners can provide technical support and troubleshooting for complex issues.

- Training and Adoption: Partners often offer training programs to help your team adopt Microsoft Lists and integrate it into your workflows seamlessly.

Summary

Utilizing Microsoft's support resources can significantly enhance your experience with Microsoft Lists, ensuring you can efficiently manage and troubleshoot any issues that arise. From comprehensive documentation and interactive learning platforms to community forums and direct support options, Microsoft provides a wide range of tools to help you succeed. By familiarizing yourself with these resources and knowing how to access them, you can make the most of Microsoft Lists and maintain smooth, organized workflows.

Joining the Microsoft Lists Community

In today's interconnected digital landscape, communities play a vital role in enhancing our knowledge and skills. The Microsoft Lists community is a rich resource for users of all levels, offering support, insights, and opportunities for collaboration. By joining this community, you can leverage collective knowledge to solve problems, share experiences, and stay updated with the latest developments.

The Benefits of Joining the Community

1. Access to Expertise and Experience

One of the primary advantages of joining the Microsoft Lists community is gaining access to a vast pool of expertise. Community members range from beginners to seasoned professionals who have encountered and overcome various challenges. This diversity means you can find answers to your questions from those who have firsthand experience.

2. Collaborative Problem Solving

When you encounter issues or need advice, the community is an excellent platform for collaborative problem-solving. By posting your questions or problems, you invite feedback and solutions from others who might have faced similar situations. This collaborative approach often leads to quicker and more effective resolutions than working in isolation.

3. Staying Informed About Updates and Best Practices

The Microsoft Lists community is also a hub for the latest news, updates, and best practices. Community members frequently share insights about new features, updates, and innovative ways to use Microsoft Lists. Staying active in the community ensures you are always informed about the latest developments and can apply best practices to your work.

4. Networking Opportunities

Joining the community provides valuable networking opportunities. You can connect with professionals in your field, participate in discussions, and even collaborate on projects. Networking within the community can open doors to new career opportunities, partnerships, and professional growth.

How to Join the Microsoft Lists Community

1. Microsoft Tech Community

The Microsoft Tech Community is the primary platform for users of Microsoft products, including Microsoft Lists. To join, follow these steps:

- Visit the Microsoft Tech Community Website: Navigate to the [Microsoft Tech Community website](https://techcommunity.microsoft.com/).

- Sign Up or Sign In: If you don't already have an account, you'll need to sign up. You can use your Microsoft account to sign in.

- Join the Microsoft Lists Community: Once you're signed in, search for the Microsoft Lists community. Join the group to start participating in discussions and accessing resources.

2. Social Media Platforms

Social media platforms like LinkedIn, Twitter, and Facebook also host active Microsoft Lists communities. These platforms offer different dynamics and engagement styles:

- LinkedIn: Search for groups related to Microsoft Lists or Microsoft 365. LinkedIn groups are great for professional networking and in-depth discussions.

- Twitter: Follow hashtags like MicrosoftLists, Microsoft365, or Office365. Twitter is ideal for quick updates, news, and connecting with experts.

- Facebook: Look for groups dedicated to Microsoft Lists. Facebook groups often have a more informal and supportive atmosphere.

3. User Forums and Discussion Boards

Apart from the official Microsoft Tech Community, other forums and discussion boards are dedicated to Microsoft Lists and Microsoft 365:

- Reddit: Subreddits like r/Office365 and r/Microsoft365 are popular places to ask questions and share knowledge.

- Stack Overflow: For more technical queries, Stack Overflow can be a valuable resource where you can ask detailed questions and get answers from experienced developers and IT professionals.

4. Webinars and Online Events

Microsoft and other organizations frequently host webinars and online events focused on Microsoft Lists. Participating in these events can provide you with the latest information, tips, and tricks directly from experts. Additionally, these events often include Q&A sessions where you can interact with presenters and other attendees.

5. Local User Groups and Meetups

If you prefer in-person interactions, look for local user groups and meetups related to Microsoft 365 or Microsoft Lists. These gatherings provide opportunities to learn from presentations, engage in discussions, and network with other professionals in your area.

Best Practices for Engaging in the Community

1. Be Respectful and Professional

When participating in community discussions, always maintain a respectful and professional tone. Remember that the community is a diverse group of individuals with varying levels of expertise and backgrounds.

2. Contribute and Share Knowledge

Communities thrive on active participation. Don't hesitate to share your knowledge and experiences. Answering questions, providing insights, and sharing your own challenges and solutions can greatly benefit others.

3. Ask Clear and Concise Questions

When seeking help, ensure your questions are clear and concise. Provide relevant details and context to help others understand your issue. This increases the chances of receiving accurate and helpful responses.

4. Follow Community Guidelines

Most communities have guidelines or rules to ensure productive and respectful interactions. Familiarize yourself with these guidelines and adhere to them to maintain a positive community environment.

5. Stay Active and Engaged

Regularly engage with the community to build relationships and stay updated. Even if you don't have immediate questions or issues, participating in discussions and following updates can provide valuable insights and learning opportunities.

Conclusion

Joining the Microsoft Lists community is a strategic move for anyone looking to maximize their use of the tool. By leveraging the collective knowledge, staying informed about updates, and engaging in collaborative problem-solving, you can enhance your productivity and efficiency with Microsoft Lists. Whether you choose to join the Microsoft Tech Community, engage on social media, participate in forums, or attend webinars, the key is to remain active and contribute to the community. In doing so, you not only benefit from the wealth of shared knowledge but also become a valuable part of a vibrant and supportive network.

8.3 Keeping Up with Updates

Keeping up with updates is essential for making the most of Microsoft Lists. Regular updates from Microsoft can introduce new features, enhance existing functionalities, and improve overall user experience. Staying informed ensures that you and your team are leveraging the latest tools and techniques to maintain efficiency and productivity.

Staying Informed About New Features

In the rapidly evolving world of technology, staying informed about new features in Microsoft Lists is crucial. Microsoft continuously updates its software to address user needs, fix bugs, and introduce innovative functionalities. Here are some effective strategies to ensure you are always up-to-date with the latest enhancements in Microsoft Lists:

1. Microsoft 365 Message Center

The Microsoft 365 Message Center is the primary source for official announcements and updates. It provides detailed information on upcoming changes, new features, and maintenance schedules. Here's how to make the most of the Message Center:

- Regular Monitoring: Regularly check the Message Center for updates. Set a weekly or bi-weekly schedule to review new messages.

- Categorization: Messages are categorized by product, making it easy to find updates specific to Microsoft Lists.

- Actionable Insights: Many messages include actions that administrators or users need to take. Ensure you follow these instructions to prepare for upcoming changes.

2. Microsoft 365 Admin Center

For those with administrative access, the Microsoft 365 Admin Center offers a comprehensive view of all updates and service health. It is a vital tool for IT administrators to manage updates and ensure smooth implementation. Key features include:

- Service Health Dashboard: Monitor the health of Microsoft Lists and other services. Any ongoing issues or outages are reported here.

- Message Center Integration: The Admin Center integrates with the Message Center, providing a unified view of all updates and alerts.

3. Microsoft Tech Community

The Microsoft Tech Community is a vibrant platform where users and experts share knowledge, discuss updates, and provide solutions. Here's how to leverage this community:

- Join Relevant Groups: Join groups and forums focused on Microsoft Lists and related technologies. Participate in discussions to stay informed.

- Follow Microsoft Experts: Follow experts and MVPs (Most Valuable Professionals) who regularly post about updates and best practices.

- Webinars and Events: Attend webinars and virtual events hosted by the community. These sessions often feature demos of new features and Q&A segments.

4. Microsoft Blogs and Announcements

Microsoft's official blogs and announcement pages are valuable resources for detailed insights into new features and updates. These blogs often include:

- In-Depth Articles: Detailed articles explaining new features, how they work, and their benefits.

- Use Cases: Real-world use cases demonstrating how to apply new functionalities effectively.

- Future Roadmaps: Insights into Microsoft's future plans for Lists, helping you anticipate upcoming changes.

5. Product Release Notes

Release notes provide a comprehensive list of all changes, improvements, and new features included in each update. Accessing these notes regularly can help you understand:

- Feature Enhancements: Detailed descriptions of new features and enhancements.

- Bug Fixes: Information on resolved issues and bugs.

- Version History: Track the version history to see how Microsoft Lists has evolved over time.

6. Microsoft Learn

Microsoft Learn offers a wide range of tutorials, courses, and learning paths to help users master new features. Utilize this platform to:

- Take Courses: Enroll in courses specifically designed for Microsoft Lists. These courses are regularly updated to reflect new features.

- Interactive Tutorials: Use interactive tutorials to get hands-on experience with new functionalities.

- Certification Programs: Consider pursuing certifications to validate your expertise and stay competitive in the job market.

7. Social Media and Newsletters

Social media platforms and newsletters are excellent ways to receive real-time updates. Follow these channels to stay informed:

- Twitter and LinkedIn: Follow official Microsoft accounts and influential industry leaders who share updates and insights.

- Newsletters: Subscribe to newsletters from Microsoft and trusted industry sources. These often include summaries of important updates and links to detailed articles.

8. User Groups and Meetups

Local user groups and meetups provide opportunities to network with other Microsoft Lists users and professionals. Participate in these events to:

- Share Experiences: Exchange experiences and tips with peers who use Microsoft Lists.

- Learn Best Practices: Learn best practices and innovative ways to use new features.

- Get Support: Receive support and advice from the community on effectively implementing updates.

9. Official Documentation

Microsoft's official documentation is a comprehensive resource for understanding new features. Regularly review the documentation to:

- Get Detailed Instructions: Find step-by-step instructions on using new features.

- Understand Technical Details: Access technical details and specifications that help in advanced configurations.

- Find FAQs: Review frequently asked questions to quickly resolve common issues.

10. Feedback and Beta Programs

Participating in feedback and beta programs allows you to experience new features before they are officially released. Engage with these programs to:

- Test New Features: Test new features in beta and provide feedback to Microsoft.

- Influence Development: Your feedback can influence the development and refinement of features.

- Early Adoption: Prepare for early adoption of features, giving your organization a competitive edge.

Staying informed about new features in Microsoft Lists ensures that you can leverage the latest tools to enhance productivity and efficiency. By utilizing these strategies, you can keep up with the continuous improvements and innovations that Microsoft brings to its Lists application. This proactive approach will not only help you stay ahead but also enable you to utilize Microsoft Lists to its full potential, ensuring seamless data management and collaboration in your organization.

Participating in Feedback Programs

Microsoft Lists is a dynamic tool that evolves with the needs of its users. Staying up-to-date with the latest features, enhancements, and fixes is crucial for maximizing the potential of Microsoft Lists in your organization. One of the most effective ways to influence the development of Microsoft Lists and stay informed about upcoming changes is by participating in Microsoft's feedback programs. These programs provide a platform for users to share their experiences, suggest improvements, and engage directly with the product development team. In this section, we will explore the various feedback programs offered by Microsoft, the benefits of participating in these programs, and how you can effectively contribute to the evolution of Microsoft Lists.

The Importance of User Feedback

User feedback is invaluable to the development of any software product. It provides developers with insights into how real users interact with the tool, what challenges they face, and what features they find most valuable. For Microsoft Lists, user feedback helps shape the roadmap of future updates, ensuring that the product evolves in ways that address the actual needs of its user base. By participating in feedback programs, users can play a direct role in the enhancement of the tool, making it more effective and user-friendly.

Types of Feedback Programs

Microsoft offers several avenues through which users can provide feedback and stay informed about product developments. These include:

1. Microsoft Insider Program

2. UserVoice

3. Microsoft Tech Community

4. Beta Testing Programs

5. Direct Feedback Through the App

Microsoft Insider Program

The Microsoft Insider Program is designed for users who want early access to new features and updates. As an Insider, you get to test pre-release versions of Microsoft Lists and other Microsoft 365 applications. This early access allows you to explore new functionalities before they are rolled out to the general public and provide feedback directly to the development team.

How to Join:

- Visit the Microsoft Insider Program website and sign up using your Microsoft account.

- Choose the level of participation (e.g., Beta Channel, Release Preview Channel) based on how early you want to access new updates.

- Download and install the Insider version of Microsoft Lists.

Benefits:

- Early access to new features and improvements.

- Opportunity to provide feedback that directly influences the development of the product.

- Access to a community of other Insiders who share insights and tips.

Providing Feedback:

- Use the Feedback Hub app to report issues and suggest improvements.

- Participate in Insider forums to discuss experiences and share feedback with other users and Microsoft engineers.

UserVoice

UserVoice is an online platform where users can submit ideas, vote on suggestions, and see what other users are requesting. It's a great way to voice your opinion and see what improvements are popular among the community.

How to Use UserVoice:

- Visit the Microsoft Lists UserVoice page.

- Submit new ideas or search for existing suggestions that align with your thoughts.

- Vote on ideas you support and leave comments to provide additional context.

Benefits:

- Transparent feedback process where you can see the status of your suggestions.

- Ability to prioritize features that matter most to you and your organization.

- Regular updates from Microsoft on the implementation of popular suggestions.

Microsoft Tech Community

The Microsoft Tech Community is a vibrant online forum where users can discuss Microsoft products, share best practices, and provide feedback. The community includes forums dedicated to Microsoft Lists, where you can engage with other users and Microsoft employees.

How to Participate:

- Join the Microsoft Tech Community by creating an account.

- Navigate to the Microsoft Lists forum.

- Participate in discussions, ask questions, and share your feedback on various topics.

Benefits:

- Engage with a broad community of Microsoft Lists users and experts.

- Get answers to your questions and solutions to problems from community members and Microsoft staff.

- Stay updated on the latest news and updates related to Microsoft Lists.

Beta Testing Programs

Microsoft occasionally runs beta testing programs for major updates or new features. These programs invite users to test new functionalities in a controlled environment and provide detailed feedback.

How to Join:

- Keep an eye on announcements from Microsoft regarding upcoming beta programs.

- Sign up for the beta testing program through the provided channels.

Benefits:

- Exclusive access to new features before their official release.

- Direct communication with the product development team.

- Influence the final implementation of new features based on your feedback.

Providing Feedback:

- Use the provided feedback tools and forms to report issues and suggest improvements.

- Participate in scheduled feedback sessions or surveys conducted by Microsoft.

Direct Feedback Through the App

Microsoft Lists includes built-in tools for providing feedback directly from within the app. This feature allows you to share your thoughts and report issues in real-time as you use the product.

How to Provide Feedback:

- Open Microsoft Lists and navigate to the settings menu.

- Select the feedback option to open the feedback tool.

- Submit your feedback, including screenshots and descriptions to provide context.

Benefits:

- Quick and convenient way to share your experiences and suggestions.

- Feedback is sent directly to the Microsoft Lists development team.

- Helps Microsoft prioritize fixes and improvements based on user reports.

Benefits of Participating in Feedback Programs

Participating in feedback programs offers numerous benefits for both individual users and organizations:

1. Influence Product Development:

   By sharing your insights and suggestions, you can help shape the future of Microsoft Lists. Your feedback can lead to the implementation of new features and improvements that address your specific needs.

2. Stay Informed About Updates:

   Feedback programs often provide participants with early access to new features and updates. This allows you to stay ahead of the curve and prepare for upcoming changes.

3. Improve Your Workflow:

   By actively participating in feedback programs, you gain a deeper understanding of Microsoft Lists and its capabilities. This knowledge can help you optimize your workflows and make the most of the tool.

4. Connect with the Community:

   Engaging in feedback programs allows you to connect with other Microsoft Lists users, share best practices, and learn from their experiences. This sense of community can be a valuable resource for troubleshooting and discovering new ways to use the tool.

5. Contribute to a Better Product:

Your feedback helps Microsoft identify and address issues, resulting in a more stable and feature-rich product. By participating in feedback programs, you contribute to the continuous improvement of Microsoft Lists for all users.

How to Provide Effective Feedback

To maximize the impact of your feedback, it's important to provide detailed, constructive, and actionable insights. Here are some tips for providing effective feedback:

1. Be Specific:

Clearly describe the issue or suggestion, including steps to reproduce the problem or specific details about the feature you're requesting.

2. Provide Context:

Explain how the issue affects your workflow or how the suggested feature would benefit your organization. This helps the development team understand the practical implications of your feedback.

3. Include Screenshots:

Visual aids such as screenshots or videos can help illustrate your point and provide additional clarity.

4. Be Constructive:

Focus on providing solutions and constructive criticism rather than just pointing out problems. Suggest how a feature could be improved or how an issue could be resolved.

5. Stay Engaged:

Follow up on your feedback, participate in discussions, and respond to any questions or requests for additional information from the development team.

Conclusion

Participating in Microsoft's feedback programs is a valuable way to stay informed about the latest updates, influence the development of Microsoft Lists, and connect with a community of users. By providing detailed and constructive feedback, you can help shape the future of Microsoft Lists, ensuring it continues to evolve in ways that meet your needs and enhance your productivity. Whether you're a casual user or a power user, your insights and experiences are crucial to the ongoing improvement of this powerful tool.

Conclusion

Summary of Key Points

Introduction

In this comprehensive guide, we have delved deep into the functionalities and features of Microsoft Lists. This summary will encapsulate the key points discussed throughout the book, serving as a quick reference for the critical aspects of Microsoft Lists. Whether you are revisiting for a quick brush-up or seeking to recall specific features, this summary aims to provide a succinct yet thorough review of the essential elements of Microsoft Lists.

Chapter 1: Getting Started with Microsoft Lists

1. Introduction to Microsoft Lists

   - Microsoft Lists is a versatile tool designed for information tracking and organization. It integrates seamlessly with other Microsoft 365 apps, enhancing productivity.

   - Key features include customizable columns, multiple view options, and robust integration capabilities.

2. Setting Up Your Microsoft Account

   - Creating a Microsoft account is the first step to accessing Microsoft Lists. Ensure your account settings are configured to maximize the integration benefits across Microsoft 365.

   - Access Microsoft Lists through the Microsoft 365 portal or directly via the Lists app on various devices.

3. Navigating the Interface

   - The interface of Microsoft Lists is user-friendly, with a main dashboard that provides easy access to all your lists and templates.

- Creating your first list involves selecting a template or starting from scratch, followed by customizing columns and views according to your needs.

Chapter 2: Creating and Managing Lists

1. Creating a New List

- Lists can be created from scratch, using templates, or by importing data from Excel or other sources.

- Templates are available for common scenarios such as issue tracking, event planning, and asset management, providing a quick start.

2. Customizing List Columns

- Customize columns to suit your data needs. Options include text, number, choice, date, and more.

- Modifying column properties and adding descriptions helps in better data categorization and user understanding.

3. Using List Views

- Views allow you to display list data in different formats such as grid, gallery, and calendar views.

- Custom views can be created to filter and sort data based on specific criteria, enhancing data visibility and usability.

Chapter 3: Advanced List Features

1. Integrating with Other Microsoft 365 Apps

- Integration with Teams, SharePoint, and Power Automate enhances collaborative workflows.

- Use Power Automate to create automated workflows that trigger actions based on list events, such as sending notifications or updating other lists.

2. Setting Up Alerts and Notifications

- Alerts can be configured to notify users of changes to list items, ensuring timely updates and action.

- Manage notifications to avoid information overload while ensuring critical updates are not missed.

3. Using Rules and Automations

- Rules enable automated actions based on conditions set for list items. Simple rules can be created directly in Microsoft Lists.

- For more complex automations, use Power Automate to design workflows that integrate with various services and applications.

Chapter 4: Collaborating with Microsoft Lists

1. Sharing Lists with Others

- Lists can be shared with individuals or groups, with permissions set to control access levels.

- Real-time collaboration is facilitated through Microsoft 365, allowing multiple users to work on lists simultaneously.

2. Commenting and Mentions

- Comments can be added to list items to facilitate discussions and feedback.

- Mentions within comments notify specific users, drawing their attention to particular items or issues.

3. Tracking Changes and Activity

- Version history allows you to track changes made to list items, revert to previous versions, and maintain a record of edits.

- Activity logs provide insights into who made changes and when, supporting accountability and transparency.

Chapter 5: Managing Data in Microsoft Lists

1. Importing and Exporting Data

- Import data from various sources such as Excel, CSV files, and other databases to quickly populate lists.

- Export list data for reporting, analysis, or backup purposes, ensuring flexibility in data handling.

2. Data Validation and Formatting

- Set up validation rules to ensure data integrity, such as requiring specific formats or restricting input ranges.

- Use formatting options to highlight important data, making lists more readable and informative.

3. Using Calculated Columns

- Calculated columns allow you to create formulas within lists, enabling dynamic data calculations.

- Practical applications include summing values, performing date calculations, and creating conditional logic within list items.

Chapter 6: Visualizing Data with Microsoft Lists

1. Creating Charts and Graphs

- Utilize built-in tools or integrate with Power BI to create visual representations of list data.

- Charts and graphs provide insights and facilitate data-driven decision-making.

2. Conditional Formatting

- Apply conditional formatting to change the appearance of list items based on specific criteria.

- Practical uses include highlighting overdue tasks, flagging high-priority items, and differentiating statuses.

3. Using Calendar and Gallery Views

- Calendar views display list items with date information in a calendar format, ideal for scheduling and tracking.

- Gallery views present list items visually, using images or other visual elements to enhance data representation.

Chapter 7: Best Practices for Microsoft Lists

1. Organizing Lists Effectively

- Use consistent naming conventions and descriptions to make lists easily identifiable and accessible.

- Categorize and tag lists to streamline organization and retrieval.

2. Maintaining Data Integrity

- Regularly audit list data to ensure accuracy and completeness.

- Implement data security measures such as access controls and permissions to protect sensitive information.

3. Tips for Efficient Workflow

- Utilize keyboard shortcuts and quick commands to navigate and manage lists efficiently.

- Apply time-saving tips and best practices to optimize your workflow and productivity with Microsoft Lists.

Chapter 8: Troubleshooting and Support

1. Common Issues and Solutions

- Address common issues such as data import problems, access errors, and performance challenges with practical solutions.

- Use troubleshooting tips to quickly resolve issues and maintain smooth list operations.

2. Accessing Help and Support

- Leverage Microsoft's support resources, including documentation, forums, and customer support, for assistance.

- Join the Microsoft Lists community to share knowledge, ask questions, and stay updated with the latest developments.

3. Keeping Up with Updates

  - Stay informed about new features and updates through Microsoft's release notes and announcements.

  - Participate in feedback programs to influence future developments and improvements in Microsoft Lists.

Conclusion

In summary, Microsoft Lists is a powerful tool for data organization and management, offering a wide range of features to enhance productivity and collaboration. By understanding and utilizing the key points discussed in this guide, users can maximize the potential of Microsoft Lists to streamline their workflows and achieve better organizational efficiency. As Microsoft continues to innovate and update its offerings, staying engaged with new features and best practices will ensure continued success with Microsoft Lists.

Future of Microsoft Lists

As organizations around the world continue to seek more efficient and effective ways to manage their data and workflows, Microsoft Lists stands out as a powerful tool that is poised to evolve and expand in numerous ways. The future of Microsoft Lists is shaped by technological advancements, user feedback, and the ever-changing landscape of digital transformation. In this section, we will explore the potential developments and trends that are likely to influence the future of Microsoft Lists, ensuring it remains an indispensable tool for businesses and individuals alike.

1. Integration with Emerging Technologies

One of the most exciting prospects for the future of Microsoft Lists is its integration with emerging technologies. As artificial intelligence (AI) and machine learning (ML) become increasingly sophisticated, Microsoft Lists will likely incorporate these technologies to enhance its capabilities. Imagine AI-driven insights that can predict trends, suggest optimizations, and automate routine tasks within your lists. Machine learning algorithms could analyze patterns in your data, providing predictive analytics that help you make more informed decisions.

Moreover, the integration of AI and ML can improve data validation and error detection, ensuring the integrity and accuracy of your lists. For instance, AI could automatically flag inconsistencies or anomalies in data entries, reducing the risk of errors and enhancing data reliability.

2. Enhanced Collaboration Features

Collaboration is at the heart of many business processes, and Microsoft Lists will continue to evolve to support seamless teamwork. Future updates may include more advanced collaboration features, such as real-time co-authoring, where multiple users can simultaneously edit and update lists. This real-time collaboration can enhance productivity and ensure that team members are always working with the most up-to-date information.

Additionally, integration with communication platforms like Microsoft Teams will likely deepen. Enhanced integration could include more intuitive ways to share lists, assign tasks, and track progress directly within Teams channels. This seamless collaboration environment will make it easier for teams to stay connected and coordinated, regardless of their physical location.

3. Increased Customization and Personalization

User feedback plays a crucial role in shaping the future of Microsoft Lists, and one area that users consistently seek improvements in is customization and personalization. Future versions of Microsoft Lists will likely offer more robust customization options, allowing users to tailor the interface and functionality to their specific needs.

This could include more flexible templates, customizable forms, and advanced scripting capabilities using tools like Power Apps and Power Automate. Users may also have the ability to create custom workflows and automation rules that align with their unique business processes. Personalization features could extend to user interfaces, enabling individuals to configure dashboards and views that prioritize the information most relevant to their roles and responsibilities.

4. Improved Mobile Experience

In an increasingly mobile world, the ability to access and manage data on the go is essential. Microsoft Lists will continue to improve its mobile experience, ensuring that users can efficiently work with lists from their smartphones and tablets. Future updates may include more responsive mobile interfaces, offline capabilities, and enhanced synchronization with desktop versions.

The improved mobile experience will empower users to stay productive and connected, regardless of their location. Whether it's updating project status during a site visit or reviewing sales data while traveling, the future of Microsoft Lists will make mobile data management more intuitive and effective.

5. Advanced Data Visualization and Reporting

Data visualization and reporting are critical for turning raw data into actionable insights. Microsoft Lists will likely expand its data visualization capabilities, offering more advanced charting, graphing, and reporting tools. Integration with Power BI, Microsoft's powerful business analytics service, could become more seamless, allowing users to create sophisticated visualizations directly from their lists.

Future enhancements may also include more interactive dashboards, where users can drill down into data, filter information, and explore trends dynamically. These advanced visualization tools will help users make sense of complex data sets and communicate insights more effectively to stakeholders.

6. Enhanced Security and Compliance

As data privacy and security concerns continue to grow, Microsoft Lists will prioritize enhanced security and compliance features. Future updates will likely include more granular access controls, ensuring that only authorized users can view or edit sensitive information. Advanced encryption methods and secure data storage solutions will protect data from unauthorized access and breaches.

Compliance with industry-specific regulations, such as GDPR, HIPAA, and CCPA, will be a key focus. Microsoft Lists will provide tools and features that help organizations maintain compliance, including audit trails, data retention policies, and regulatory reporting capabilities. These enhancements will give users peace of mind, knowing that their data is secure and compliant with relevant laws and standards.

7. Integration with the Internet of Things (IoT)

The Internet of Things (IoT) is transforming the way businesses collect and analyze data. Microsoft Lists has the potential to integrate with IoT devices, enabling real-time data collection and management. For example, sensors and devices in a manufacturing plant could automatically update lists with production metrics, equipment status, and maintenance schedules.

This real-time integration will provide organizations with a more comprehensive view of their operations, allowing them to respond quickly to changes and optimize processes. The future of Microsoft Lists will harness the power of IoT to drive smarter, data-driven decision-making.

8. Expanded Use Cases and Applications

As Microsoft Lists continues to evolve, its use cases and applications will expand across various industries and domains. From project management and inventory tracking to customer relationship management and compliance monitoring, Microsoft Lists will adapt to meet the diverse needs of users.

Future developments may include industry-specific templates and solutions, tailored to the unique requirements of sectors such as healthcare, finance, manufacturing, and education. These specialized applications will make it easier for organizations to implement Microsoft Lists and realize its full potential in their specific contexts.

9. Community-Driven Innovations

The Microsoft community is a vibrant ecosystem of users, developers, and partners who contribute to the continuous improvement of Microsoft products. The future of Microsoft Lists will be shaped by community-driven innovations, with users sharing best practices, templates, and custom solutions.

Microsoft will likely continue to support and foster this community through forums, user groups, and events. By listening to user feedback and incorporating community-driven ideas, Microsoft Lists will remain a dynamic and evolving tool that addresses the real-world challenges faced by its users.

10. Continuous Improvement and Regular Updates

Microsoft is committed to the continuous improvement of its products, and Microsoft Lists is no exception. Users can expect regular updates that introduce new features, enhancements, and bug fixes. These updates will be driven by user feedback, technological advancements, and market trends.

Microsoft's agile development approach ensures that Microsoft Lists remains responsive to the needs of its users. Whether it's through monthly updates or major annual releases, the future of Microsoft Lists will be marked by a steady stream of improvements that enhance usability, functionality, and performance.

Conclusion

The future of Microsoft Lists is bright, with numerous exciting developments on the horizon. As it continues to integrate with emerging technologies, enhance collaboration, and offer more customization options, Microsoft Lists will solidify its position as a vital tool for data management and workflow optimization.

By staying attuned to user feedback and leveraging the power of the Microsoft ecosystem, Microsoft Lists will evolve to meet the changing needs of organizations and individuals. Whether you're a business professional, a project manager, or a data enthusiast, the future of Microsoft Lists promises to deliver innovative solutions that help you stay organized, productive, and informed.

As we look ahead, we can be confident that Microsoft Lists will remain a cornerstone of digital transformation, empowering users to harness the power of their data and achieve their goals with greater efficiency and effectiveness.

Encouragement for Continued Learning

Microsoft Lists is an incredibly powerful tool, but like any technology, its full potential is only realized through continuous learning and exploration. The digital landscape is constantly evolving, and staying updated with the latest features, best practices, and integrations can significantly enhance your productivity and efficiency. This section aims to inspire and guide you in your journey of continued learning with Microsoft Lists.

1. Embrace a Growth Mindset

The first step towards continued learning is adopting a growth mindset. Understand that mastery is a journey, not a destination. Each new feature, update, or integration presents an opportunity to enhance your skills and workflows. Embrace challenges as opportunities for growth and view each problem as a chance to learn something new.

2. Leverage Microsoft's Learning Resources

Microsoft offers a wealth of resources to help you stay informed and proficient with Microsoft Lists. Here are some key resources to explore:

- Microsoft Learn: This is Microsoft's comprehensive learning platform that offers guided paths, modules, and certifications on various Microsoft products, including Microsoft Lists. The interactive nature of the platform helps reinforce learning through hands-on exercises and real-world scenarios.

- Microsoft Documentation: The official Microsoft Lists documentation is a treasure trove of information, providing detailed explanations, step-by-step guides, and best practices. Regularly reviewing the documentation can help you stay abreast of new features and changes.

- Webinars and Workshops: Microsoft frequently hosts webinars and workshops covering new features, updates, and best practices. Participating in these events can provide insights directly from Microsoft experts and offer opportunities for live Q&A sessions.

3. Join the Microsoft Tech Community

The Microsoft Tech Community is a vibrant online community where users can share knowledge, ask questions, and collaborate on solutions. Joining the community offers several benefits:

- Forums: The forums are a great place to ask questions, share your knowledge, and learn from the experiences of others. You can find discussions on a wide range of topics, from basic usage to advanced customization.

- Blogs: Microsoft experts and community members regularly post blogs with tips, tricks, and updates. Following these blogs can help you stay informed about the latest developments and gain practical insights.

- User Groups: Many regions have local Microsoft user groups that meet regularly, either in person or virtually. These groups provide a platform to network with peers, share experiences, and learn from each other.

4. Explore Third-Party Training and Certifications

In addition to Microsoft's resources, many third-party providers offer training and certifications that can enhance your expertise in Microsoft Lists and related technologies:

- Online Courses: Platforms like Udemy, Coursera, and LinkedIn Learning offer courses on Microsoft Lists and other Microsoft 365 applications. These courses are often created by industry experts and can provide a structured learning path.

- Certifications: Earning certifications from recognized institutions can validate your skills and knowledge. Certifications not only boost your credibility but also demonstrate your commitment to continuous learning and professional development.

5. Practice Continuous Improvement

Apply the principles of continuous improvement to your use of Microsoft Lists. Regularly review your workflows and processes to identify areas for improvement. Seek feedback from colleagues and stakeholders to understand how Lists can better meet their needs.

Experiment with new features and integrations to streamline your operations and enhance productivity.

6. Stay Updated with Industry Trends

The field of digital productivity is rapidly evolving, with new tools and methodologies emerging regularly. Staying updated with industry trends can provide fresh perspectives and innovative ideas to incorporate into your use of Microsoft Lists:

- Industry Publications: Subscribe to industry publications, blogs, and newsletters that cover digital productivity, project management, and collaboration tools. These sources often highlight new trends, case studies, and best practices.

- Conferences and Events: Attending industry conferences and events, either in person or virtually, can provide valuable networking opportunities and expose you to the latest innovations and thought leadership.

7. Engage in Hands-On Projects

One of the best ways to deepen your understanding and mastery of Microsoft Lists is through hands-on projects. Apply what you've learned in real-world scenarios to reinforce your skills and discover new applications:

- Personal Projects: Create personal projects to explore features and functionalities that you might not use in your professional role. This experimentation can lead to new insights and innovative uses.

- Volunteer Work: Offer your expertise to non-profit organizations or community groups. Helping them organize their data and workflows with Microsoft Lists not only benefits the organization but also provides practical experience and challenges.

- Collaborative Projects: Work on collaborative projects with colleagues or peers from the Microsoft Tech Community. These projects can provide diverse perspectives and enhance your problem-solving skills.

8. Mentor and Teach Others

Teaching others is one of the most effective ways to solidify your own understanding. As you become more proficient with Microsoft Lists, consider mentoring colleagues or conducting training sessions:

- Mentorship: Offer to mentor new users of Microsoft Lists in your organization. Share your knowledge, provide guidance, and help them navigate challenges.

- Training Sessions: Conduct training sessions or workshops for your team. Developing training materials and explaining concepts to others will reinforce your own understanding and highlight areas where you can improve.

- Content Creation: Write blogs, create video tutorials, or develop guides on Microsoft Lists. Sharing your knowledge with a broader audience not only helps others but also establishes you as a subject matter expert.

9. Reflect on Your Learning Journey

Periodically reflect on your learning journey to recognize your progress and set new goals. Consider maintaining a learning journal to document your experiences, challenges, and achievements. Reflection helps reinforce learning, identify gaps, and plan for future growth.

10. Stay Curious and Open-Minded

Finally, cultivate a mindset of curiosity and openness. Technology is constantly evolving, and there is always something new to learn. Stay curious about how Microsoft Lists can be used in different contexts and industries. Be open to new ideas, and don't be afraid to step outside your comfort zone.

Conclusion

Continued learning is essential to fully harness the power of Microsoft Lists and stay ahead in the dynamic world of digital productivity. By leveraging available resources, engaging with the community, and maintaining a growth mindset, you can continually enhance your skills and contribute to more efficient and effective workflows. Remember, the journey of mastering Microsoft Lists is ongoing, and each step forward brings new opportunities for discovery and improvement.

Glossary of Terms

1. List

  - Definition: A fundamental component of Microsoft Lists, allowing users to organize and manage data in a structured format. Lists consist of rows (items) and columns (fields), providing flexibility in data storage and retrieval.

2. Column

  - Definition: An individual data field within a list, used to store specific types of information such as text, numbers, dates, or choices. Columns can be customized to suit different data management needs.

3. View

  - Definition: A user-defined way of displaying list data, offering various layouts and filtering options. Views in Microsoft Lists include standard, calendar, gallery, and grid views, each tailored for different data visualization purposes.

4. Template

  - Definition: Pre-configured lists with predefined structures and settings, designed to streamline the creation of common data management tasks. Templates in Microsoft Lists cover a range of use cases such as task tracking, issue management, and inventory tracking.

5. Power Automate

  - Definition: A workflow automation tool integrated with Microsoft Lists, allowing users to automate repetitive tasks and processes. Power Automate enables seamless interaction between lists and other Microsoft 365 applications.

6. SharePoint Integration

  - Definition: Integration of Microsoft Lists with SharePoint, providing advanced capabilities for data management, security, and collaboration. SharePoint integration enhances the scalability and customization options of Lists.

7. Conditional Formatting

  - Definition: A feature in Microsoft Lists that allows users to visually highlight data based on specified criteria. Conditional formatting enhances data interpretation by applying color codes and icons to emphasize important information.

8. Collaboration

  - Definition: The ability of multiple users to work simultaneously on a list, enabling real-time updates, comments, and notifications. Collaboration features in Microsoft Lists enhance teamwork and communication within organizations.

9. Data Validation

  - Definition: Rules and criteria applied to list columns to ensure data accuracy and consistency. Data validation helps prevent errors by validating user input against predefined conditions.

10. Version History

  - Definition: A record of changes made to list items over time, enabling users to track and revert to previous versions if necessary. Version history provides transparency and accountability in data management.

11. SharePoint Lists

  - Definition: Lists created and managed within SharePoint Online, offering enhanced capabilities for enterprise-level data management and integration with SharePoint sites and workflows.

12. Mobile Access

  - Definition: The ability to access and interact with Microsoft Lists using mobile devices, facilitating productivity and collaboration on the go. Mobile access ensures flexibility and responsiveness in data management tasks.

Acknowledgments

We would like to express our heartfelt gratitude to all the readers who have chosen to embark on this journey with us through "Mastering Microsoft Lists: A Comprehensive Guide." Your decision to explore the depths of Microsoft Lists reflects a commitment to enhancing organizational efficiency and embracing innovative solutions.

First and foremost, we extend our deepest thanks to Microsoft Corporation for developing Microsoft Lists and continuously advancing its capabilities. Their dedication to empowering users with tools for effective data management has made this guide possible.

We are immensely grateful to our team of contributors, whose expertise and insights have enriched every chapter of this book. Their meticulous attention to detail and passion for clarity have ensured that each topic is thoroughly explored and comprehensively explained.

To our editors and reviewers, thank you for your diligent efforts in refining the content and ensuring its accuracy. Your commitment to excellence has been invaluable in shaping this guide into a reliable resource for mastering Microsoft Lists.

Special thanks go to our families and loved ones for their unwavering support and understanding throughout the writing process. Your encouragement has been a constant source of motivation.

Last but not least, to you, our readers, we sincerely appreciate your trust and enthusiasm. It is our hope that "Mastering Microsoft Lists: A Comprehensive Guide" equips you with the knowledge and skills to leverage Microsoft Lists effectively in your daily workflows.

Thank you for choosing this book. Your journey to mastering Microsoft Lists begins here.

Warm regards,